WITHDRAWN BY THE
UNIVERSITY OF MICHIGAN

Selling the President, 1920

Selling the President, 1920

Albert D. Lasker, Advertising, and the Election of Warren G. Harding

John A. Morello

Westport, Connecticut
London

Grad
JK
526
1920
.M67
2001

Library of Congress Cataloging-in-Publication Data

Morello, John A., 1951–
  Selling the president, 1920 : Albert D. Lasker, advertising, and the election of Warren G. Harding / John A. Morello.
    p. cm.
  Includes bibliographical references and index.
  ISBN 0–275–97030–2 (alk. paper)
  1. Presidents—United States—Election—1920. 2. Advertising, Political—United States. 3. Lasker, Albert Davis, 1880–1952. I. Title.
  JK526 2001
  324.973′0913—dc21   00–064944

British Library Cataloguing in Publication Data is available.

Copyright © 2001 by John A. Morello

All rights reserved. No portion of this book may be reproduced, by any process or technique, without the express written consent of the publisher.

Library of Congress Catalog Card Number: 00–064944
ISBN: 0–275–97030–2

First published in 2001

Praeger Publishers, 88 Post Road West, Westport, CT 06881
An imprint of Greenwood Publishing Group, Inc.
www.praeger.com

Printed in the United States of America

The paper used in this book complies with the Permanent Paper Standard issued by the National Information Standards Organization (Z39.48–1984).

10 9 8 7 6 5 4 3 2 1

To Ruth: Your sacrifice made all of this possible. Thank you.

Contents

Acknowledgments ix

Abbreviations xi

Introduction 1

1. Season of Change 3

2. Albert Lasker and "Reason Why" Advertising 15

3. Pork, Beans, and Politics 27

4. To Washington, Through Chicago 37

5. Something Old, Something New . . . 49

6. Something Borrowed . . . 63

7. The Man with the Best Told Story Wins 75

8. November 2, 1920: Closing the Sale 91

Epilogue 99

References 103

Index 109

Acknowledgments

It has been said that success has a thousand fathers, but that failure is an orphan. Should this work prove to be a success, then it would be the former and not the latter. I had quite a bit of help bringing this project to paper, and the names of those who helped could quite literally fill a book. Here are just a few.

First and always to my wife Ruth, whose belief in me at times exceeded mine and whose sacrifices made mine seem small by comparison. My sister-in-law, Sharon, gave me office space in her home where a good deal of this work was written. She has a garden that proved to be a continuous source of inspiration. Drs. Richard Jensen, Leo Schelbert, and Jerry Danzer, professors at the University of Illinois at Chicago, have all played a role in helping this work take shape, and for that I am in your collective debt. Marianne Berger, Lalu Palamatan, and a legion of reference librarians across the country deserve my thanks for their assistance and their patience. The reference librarians at the Ohio Historical Society and the Indiana State Library were especially helpful in providing critical primary source documents essential to this project. The organizers of the 1999 Ohio Valley History Conference, the 1999 Illinois State History Symposium, and the 2000 Missouri Valley History Conference are all to be thanked for allowing me to present slices of this work to colleagues for their consideration. Their comments have helped to sharpen its focus. Dr. Sandra Graham, Dean of the General Education Department at the DeVry Institute of Technology in Addison, Illinois, has supported this project from its inception and approved my request for a sabbatical. William Hughes, former Dean of Academic Affairs at that same institution, first suggested that I pursue this project, and his successor, Susan Friedberg, Ph.D., has followed in his footsteps. My students at DeVry also deserve a word of thanks. Frequently my class discussions would somehow wander into a discussion of the work I was doing. They didn't seem to mind. They were genuinely interested in what I was doing, and that support kept me going when I found myself stymied either by insufficient research materials, or simply writer's block. I hope that if I've taught them anything, it's that persistence has its own rewards. When I needed assistance in preparing the final copy, David Child was a great help.

Professionally I owe Cynthia Harris at Greenwood Publishing a debt of gratitude for picking my idea out of a pile of others and giving it life. She probably wasn't looking for something like this when I stopped by her booth at the 1999 American Historical Association Convention, but she was willing to take a chance and I appreciate that. The other people that I have met at Greenwood have been equally professional, courteous, and helpful.

To the people who, for one reason or another, said this would never happen, or said they would help but never did, or in some other way chose to make this project more difficult, you too have my thanks. You were, unknowingly, a source of inspiration, and I have used the bricks you've thrown at me to build a firm foundation for the future.

Finally to my children Rebecca, Adam, and Max. Nothing is out of reach if you really want it and are willing to stretch for it.

Abbreviations

DNC   Democratic National Committee

FCBR   Foote, Cone & Belding Register

GOP   Grand Old Party (nickname for Republican Party)

RNC   Republican National Committee

Introduction

Modern advertising moved into the 20th century borne on many vehicles and many techniques. Three of the most often-used advertising strategies were "reason why" advertising, which compared similar products and gave consumers hardheaded, nononsense reasons why they should buy a certain product; testimonials, which featured celebrity endorsements; and preemptive claims, which touted a quality or process common to similar products as being unique to only that brand. Albert Davis Lasker, president of the Lord & Thomas advertising agency, championed all three advertising techniques in the early 20th century, although he was best known for his work in promoting the "reason why" style. He helped such clients as Lucky Strike cigarettes, Sunkist oranges, and Van Camp pork and beans become business success stories, and he became a wealthy man as a result.

It was quite by accident that Lasker found himself thrust into the political arena. His work on behalf of Van Camp Pork and Beans of Indiana brought him to the attention of state Republican leaders, and in particular, Republican Party (also known as the GOP, or Grand Old Party) Chairman Will Hays, soon to become chairman of the Republican National Committee (RNC). Hays needed someone to promote the Republican cause in the 1918 congressional elections. Lasker helped the GOP attack the Democratic Party for its handling and mismanagement of World War I, President Woodrow Wilson's plan for a League of Nations, and his appeal to voters to give the Democratic Party control of Congress. Lasker used "reason why" advertising to compare Wilson's plea with something akin to dictatorship ("one man rule"), which helped to unite Progressive and Old Guard Republicans. The GOP victory in November reduced the majority Democrats enjoyed in the House of Representatives and eliminated their control of the Senate altogether. Lasker also used his advertising skills to fight the battle of the League of Nations going on inside the GOP, and later on in the 1920 presidential campaign.

The November 1918 congressional victory positioned the GOP to recapture the presidency in 1920. Lasker, though initially drawn to Senator Hiram Johnson because of his anti-League views, settled, reluctantly, on Warren G. Harding after he received the nomination. As an assistant RNC chairman in charge of publicity, Lasker found himself plying his trade for a candidate he was not sure felt as strongly about the League of Nations as he did. Nonetheless he used all his advertising techniques—reason why, testimonials, and even preemptive advertising—for Harding. He turned Harding, who was not widely known outside his home state of Ohio, into a national figure, using not only advertising techniques but also communication technologies, such as motion pictures, sound recording, and wire photography, which by 1920 were being embraced by Americans in record numbers. He helped to humanize Harding, making him someone to whom average Americans could relate. He also took steps to manipulate events in Harding's life that most American voters could not relate to, that is, his marital infidelity, and allegations that he was part African-American.

Harding's victory in 1920 was not only a testimonial to the message Republicans communicated to voters that year but also to the role advertising in general, and Albert Lasker in particular, played in helping to deliver that message.

1
Season of Change

The changes began from the moment the sun peeked over the horizon. The Weather Bureau had promised change, and this time it was right on the money. Winds coming out of the northwest brought clearing skies and near freezing temperatures, so residents of Washington, D.C., reached for their coats as they made their way out the door on the morning of March 4, 1921.[1] The change in the weather was the latest event in what had become a season of change. March 4th was Inauguration Day, the day Warren G. Harding would replace Woodrow Wilson and become the twenty-ninth president of the United States and the first Republican president since 1912. Harding's ascendancy marked an end to eight years of Democratic control of the White House and was the crowning achievement for the Grand Old Party (GOP). The GOP had nearly imploded a decade earlier over internal squabbles, but the party had since changed from an amalgam of fractious state and regional interests to a cohesive, nationally run organization ready to take the United States in a different direction. The country was ready, and had been for some time. As the nation prepared to inaugurate Harding, he was about to take charge of a country that was very different than it had been under Woodrow Wilson's administration. The United States was larger and more crowded; the total area exceeded 3 million square miles, and the population stood at over 106 million, a majority of whom now lived in cities.[2] Most lived in the East and the Upper Midwest, although some were drifting west to California, and as a result the state doubled its population between 1900 and 1920. Americans in 1920 were older, mostly white, and mostly male. Additionally the number of women and minorities, especially African-Americans, had increased. In the case of African-Americans, numbers told only half the story as they had been on the move since 1900, heading north to such places as Chicago and Detroit. In 1920 women and African-Americans would play a role in the changing the political leadership of the country, just as their physical presence had changed the nation's demographic identity.

In addition to demographic changes, there were other things that set Americans in 1920 apart from other generations. They were, on the whole, healthier, thanks to a diet featuring more fruits and vegetables and less meat. They were also better educated; literacy was up, even among nonwhite Americans, and the rates of secondary school attendance and graduation had also climbed. More people were working. The year 1920 saw manufacturing jobs gain ground on those in farming, and the general labor force was a patchwork quilt of workers: black, white, men, women, young, old. And although more Americans were working than ever in 1920, they were putting in less time on the job. Work weeks had decreased to 51 hours in manufacturing, while at the same time paychecks had increased, especially in the areas of construction, mining, and transportation.[3] With money came product consumption and leisure time. There were 8 million registered automobiles in the United States in 1920, and that meant more roads and bridges to accommodate them and more housing to satisfy the desires of motorists who wished to escape to the suburbs. Railroads also felt the surge of prosperity, laying nearly twice as much track and carrying more than twice the number of passengers it had in 1900. And if using the telephone was indeed the next best thing to being there, Americans in 1920 took advantage of the technology in record numbers. Fifty million daily local calls were made that year from over 13 million telephones. The rate of news traveling over telephone wires ran neck and neck with news in black and white, as newspaper circulation also boomed. The introduction of radio and the expansion of airmail capabilities would soon make 1920 look like the dawn of the first modern information age.

Many of the new technological changes would figure greatly in the political changes unfolding at the White House in March 1921. The Republican Party made extensive use of the telephone, the movie camera, and the ability to electronically transmit photographs during the fall campaign. It identified potential voters and directed specific campaign appeals to them. It also employed the services of a professional advertiser, Albert D. Lasker of Chicago's Lord & Thomas advertising agency, to help promote Warren Harding in the same way soap, milk, or beer might be handled.

Yet not all the changes, be they political, technological, or social, were being embraced by Americans. In fact the decision by voters in November 1920 to exchange a Democrat for a Republican president reflected in many cases their concern with the changes underway in the country, many of them coming quickly after 1918. Americans had tried to signal their concerns about the changes going on; they sought direction from those in charge. Unfortunately Woodrow Wilson, preoccupied by international affairs and later incapacitated by a stroke, found himself either unwilling or unable to grasp or come to grips with the changes going on. His insistence on being exclusively responsible for policies, as one observer put it, turned his administration into a one-man show, and once he was slowed by a stroke, the entire government ground to a halt. The plight the United States found itself in, in 1920 seemed to some to resemble a ship at sea with its engines stopped, with no one on the bridge or in the engine room able to fix the problem. Whatever the reason, the changes taking place between 1918 and 1920 were on their own jarring enough to warrant a change in national leadership.

The sudden end of World War I caught many Americans in and out of power by surprise. Even though the Armistice was cause for national celebration, including the illumination of the Capitol Dome in Washington, D.C., little thought had been given as to what to do after the shooting and the cheering stopped.[4] There were over 2 million Americans serving in the armed forces at the time the war ended, and they wanted to come home. They returned to a country grateful to have them back, but unprepared on how to effectively turn them back into civilians. Veterans came home expecting to pick up where they left off, only to find a world very different from the one they left. Many became disillusioned and disappointed, and by 1920, they were ready to vote their frustrations.

Those frustrations were further aggravated as the nation's economy took a long time to change from a wartime to a peacetime footing. In the absence of a national plan, solutions at the state and local level were implemented. The results were chaotic. Unions wanted the benefits and protection enjoyed during the wartime economy, while business called for an end to government interference. Wilson's decision to dismantle such wartime agencies as the War Industries Board and the Food Administration only added to the confusion.[5] The result seemed to be an economy out of control. Unions lost members as the economy slowed down, and went on strike to protest. Unemployment went from 1.4 percent in 1918 to 4 percent in 1920, and then shot to nearly 12 percent by 1921. Farmers saw prices for their goods fall, while consumers suffered sticker shock every time they went to the supermarket. Inflation flared up, investment capital dried up, and bankruptcies went up.[6]

Some of the changes between 1918 and 1920 were more psychological than numerical. Strides made by women and African-Americans were changing the face of America. Like men, women had gone to war in 1917 and had done a lot for their country and themselves. They had raised money, campaigned for food conservation, entered the military in noncombat situations, and joined the workforce to fill the jobs men left vacant. Although postwar economic depression erased some women from employment rosters, the impression the experience left was indelible. Wilson, recognizing women's contribution, endorsed the suffrage movement early in 1918, and Congress followed his lead eighteen months later. By August 1920 women had the vote and would use it in November.

African-Americans traveled a similar path. Between 350,000 and 400,000 blacks served in the armed forces during World War I, while 500,000 went north to look for wartime jobs. American society found their services to be of value, but was reluctant to grant them rights commensurate with their contributions. The experience of African-Americans both in and out of uniform led to militancy. After the war they demanded equal treatment before the law, equal job opportunities, and equal pay. Their change in attitude upset the status quo and led to racial tensions, which exploded in several incidents in 1919.

Prohibition was another social change for which Americans were largely unprepared. In less than a month after adoption by Congress in 1918, the Eighteenth Amendment, prohibiting the manufacture, transportation, and sale of liquor in the United States, had been ratified by thirty-six states. The amendment reflected the growing rural-urban tension resulting from increasing urbanization and industrialization of the country.⁷ It was not popular, despite claims by its supporters, and it was opposed, especially in the cities.

Changes in immigration helped send Americans into emotional convulsions as the nation sought to fend off outside efforts to undermine the country. The Red Scare promoted nativism, added to social stress, and confirmed the hostility of many Americans toward minority groups. It caused some to wonder if the war to save the world for democracy had been won abroad but was being lost at home. Although the experience, which included strikes, government intervention, harassment of elected officials whose loyalties were suspect, and the deportation or imprisonment of those considered dangerous to national security, was brief, it helped set yet another precedent which promoted intolerance and encouraged conformity.⁸

Sobered by war, disillusioned by the changes peace brought, and annoyed at the intrusive nature of its government at home and abroad, Americans in 1919 and 1920 looked to their leaders, and especially their president, for leadership. But it was not to be found. Despite reassurances from Washington that the problems the country was going through would solve themselves, they weren't going away fast enough to suit voters. The power of the presidency, at least in Wilson's hands, seemed to be dissolving. Congress appeared distracted by political infighting and Red Scare witch-hunting. The economy was a mess, entangled with government regulation, and no one seemed to be listening. Voters ultimately decided to introduce some changes of their own, slowing the country down, steering it off the global highway it had been traveling since 1914 and back to less busy streets. At the time Warren G. Harding seemed to be the perfect guide. A small town newspaper owner from Ohio, he seemed to be living proof that nice guys could finish first. A politician who seemed to put people first, and valued friendship and loyalty above all else, he was portrayed to Americans as someone who shared their weariness with the passions of war, intraparty strife, and the high-brow intellectualism symbolized by Woodrow Wilson. He would change the nation back to what it had been before World War I, before the Armistice, before the federal government had swollen in size—back to normalcy. Harding's campaign rarely strayed from those themes, and Harding himself rarely strayed from the front porch of his home in Marion, Ohio. Voters came to him the way the faithful would pilgrimage to some religious site. He met them on the steps of his house and promised them a return to normalcy. However, the change Harding promised voters was just one of several changes made during this campaign. While he stayed on his porch, supporters fanned out across the nation to spread his message. The GOP had embraced the changes in technology that had occurred since 1910, and used them to put a favorable impression of Harding in the mind of the voters who couldn't make the trek to Marion. Photos, movie clips, sound recordings, and billboards all announced the coming of change. In fact Harding's presidential campaign was the first time photography was manipulated as a campaign tool. Shots of Harding, his wife Florence, and the visitors to their home were the prototype of today's commonly known photo opportunity. They were taken by the thousands, sorted out by Republican National Headquarters, and then distributed to newspapers and magazines nationwide in an attempt to show Americans that the Hardings were like them: just plain folks.⁹ Modern advertising and modern politics were about to forge an alliance during this campaign, and the anniversary of such a merger would be observed for years to come. Albert Lasker would lend his skills to the packaging and sale of a president, using commercial gimmicks to convey a political message. Whether voters were responding to the hangover of war, the danger of future conflicts, or the problems of the economy as it changed from a wartime to peacetime footing, the messages were wrapped in commercial advertising. The results were undeniable. Republicans had tightened their hold on the Congress and had now won the White House for the first time since 1912.

Perhaps it was the speed and severity of change that figured into the planning for Warren Harding's inauguration in Washington, D.C., that frosty March morning. Almost from the moment the votes had been counted, supporters had hoped his inaugural would be a chance to release the energy and frustrations that had been pent-up since the beginning of World War I. Ned McLean, publisher of the *Washington Post* and a Harding supporter, had been named a cochair of the Inaugural Committee, and he had big plans. He envisioned an event about ten times as lively as the Fourth of July combined with the ending of a victorious war.[10] Harding made it known that the ceremonies marking the change in watch from Wilson's to his should be subdued, in keeping with the nation's mood. The Senate Committee on Arrangements, led by Henry Cabot Lodge, made plans for an inaugural that would be dignified, subdued, and, of course, sober.[11] The proceedings would be long on substance but short on ceremony. No lavish parties, no street celebrations, not even a parade after Harding was sworn in.[12] But at the very least, most people expected the arrival of the Hardings and the departure of the Wilsons would bring some changes to life in Washington. The stiff, formal Wilsonian decorum would be replaced by Harding folksiness. Children would soon be able to take part in the revived Easter Egg hunts on the White House lawn. People who passed Secret Service inspection could soon drop by the White House during the lunch hour and shake hands with the president. The sound of music would soon return to 1600 Pennsylvania Avenue, as the Hardings resurrected another tradition shelved by Wilson, the weekly Marine Band concerts.[13] Even the White House itself was due for a changeover; the *New York Times* reported the estate would be redecorated and new furnishings added, including new flower beds around the building's perimeter.[14] Even more changes were planned. Mrs. Harding, the first woman to ever vote for her husband for president and the first First Lady to have her own Secret Service detail, would soon make some changes to her new position. She had played an important role in seeing her husband elected by working to win the votes of women. Now she would go a step further in shaping events. Julia Summers of the "Woman's Made in America League" hoped that as First Lady Mrs. Harding would wear American-made clothes, unlike Mrs. Wilson who wore gowns by Worth of Paris. For a while she became a fashion statement, sporting American dresses in a color soon to be dubbed Harding Blue.[15] She seemed to be changing the direction women wanted to be going. She established a presence for herself that was independent of her husband's, and the time she spent in the public eye unshaded by his presence did wonders for her image and that of women in general.

If Washington and the rest of the nation were asked to demonstrate restraint for the upcoming inaugural, the president-elect was also up to the challenge. Harding, who had served in the U.S. Senate since 1914, chose not to become a regular fixture on the Washington scene until just a few days before the inaugural. A trip to Panama took up most of his time after the election, and the first two months of the new year were spent vacationing in Florida, where he fished, golfed, and tended to the business of being a president-elect.

Harding sought to economize government, changing it from its bloated shape to one more in keeping with public expectations. By 1918 there were 900,000 civilians working in the federal government, more than twice the number in 1916.[16] Harding wanted a smaller, less intrusive government, and cabinet members who would help him get it. The appointments of Charles Evans Hughes as secretary of state, Henry Wallace at agriculture, Andrew Mellon at treasury, John Weeks as secretary of war, and Edwin Denby as Navy secretary were good political selections, designed to acknowledge the efforts of specific interest groups in the November election. James Davis as secretary of labor and Will Hays as postmaster general perhaps best reflected Harding's intention to cut the size of government.

Just as wartime intervention had changed the relationship between government and business, the same had occurred between government and labor. After the war labor had protested the economic problems that had resulted in the loss of wages and jobs. Harding and the GOP wanted someone to placate labor. James Davis was a former ironworker who still had his union card. Labor organizations liked the move, and Davis was appointed. Will Hays's appointment as postmaster general was in return for his service as GOP national chairman during Harding's presidential campaign. It was seen as something of a traditional move, because the postmaster general could be expected to award jobs to the party faithful. However, Hays's view that jobs should be awarded on the basis of merit and not loyalty kept the levels of patronage down in keeping with Harding's vision of a change in government.

Harding's choices of Albert Fall as secretary of the interior and Harry Daugherty as attorney general had their own unique implications on the shape of government. Fall changed public perception that a cabinet member could never go to prison, and Daugherty undermined the public's belief that the nation's chief law enforcement official should be above criminal activity. However, Harding's second-tier appointments did reflect his desire to reduce the size of government while simultaneously making it more inclusive.

Albert Lasker was placed in charge of the Shipping Board, a post he neither sought or wanted.[17] He was charged with getting the government out of the shipping business and jettisoning over one thousand ships the United States had acquired during World War I.

Women and African-Americans had added an element of change in the 1920 presidential election, so not surprisingly their presence changed the face of the government Harding was trying to assemble. Wilson, in deference to southern whites, had barred African-Americans from government positions. Harding slowly changed that, naming them as assistants to the attorney general, collectors of internal revenue, and later a minister to Liberia.[18] Women had more cause for hope as Harding rewarded their political support. A woman was named to the Civil Service Commission, and another was placed in charge of the Department of

Labor's Children's Bureau. Harding refused to fire women workers in government on the grounds they were married, and he allowed them to join the Foreign Service. He had responded to the change in status of the women's movement brought about by suffrage and was acting accordingly. Women could find no real cause for complaint regarding the treatment they received during the Harding administration.[19]

Harding also used his vacation to work on his inaugural address. The speech would underscore his intention to settle the problems war had made, but Woodrow Wilson had left untreated. Normal business and labor patterns had been disrupted by the conflict; those must be changed. Government had grown large, intrusive, and inefficient. Harding would promise to reduce its size, and increase its efficiency, operating it more as a business. He would promise tax relief and promote sound commercial practices. After years of what seemed to many Americans to be radical behavior by government, Harding promised a return to orthodoxy. The days of Roosevelt and Wilson were over, and the days of McKinley had returned.[20]

The preliminary work done, Harding returned by train to Marion on February 28th. His hometown and his neighbors had undergone quite a few changes themselves since the 1920 campaign. Marion had become a political nerve center of sorts, besieged by party faithful coming to see the candidate, as well as a national press corps charged with reporting every moment. It had had the effect of shaking the cobwebs off this small town, and had shed light on many dark places. Now the election was over, and they were left to survey the costs of change. The city would never quite regain its small town charm. However, one of the larger costs of change would be the loss of their favorite son. "Warn," "W.G.," or whatever other nickname they knew Harding by before the election, that was all over, and it was time to say good-bye to the man who lived on Mount Vernon Avenue.[21] After reassuring well-wishers that his service as president would mirror his service as lieutenant governor and later senator from Ohio, Harding and his entourage, consisting mostly of family and friends, left Marion by train on Wednesday night, March 2nd. His private car was dubbed *Superb*, which he had used during the presidential campaign. It featured electric fans, an intercom to summon staff members, and telephone service.[22] Harding's last prepresidential train journey would take him through Ohio and Pennsylvania, and then through Maryland, arriving in Washington, D.C., at around 1:30 Thursday afternoon.

As Harding sped through the night, first east and then south, the season of change was everywhere around him, even preceding him. Despite plans for a subdued inauguration, the United States was about to get a new president, and the change in leadership was becoming a frame around which other changes could be placed, or at least justified. The dome of the Capitol was going to be illuminated in Harding's honor, something that hadn't been done since the end of World War I.[23] A sound system would be used for the first time to amplify the inaugural address. Engineers from the American Telephone and Telegraph Corporation were installing it in the small kiosk built on the steps of the Capitol.[24] The publishers of the *New York Times* were making plans to fly special commemorative issues of their paper into Washington. Thirteen hundred copies would leave a Long Island airport on Inauguration day, and arrive in College Park, Maryland, two and a half hours later. The trip would be done in half the time it would take to go by train.[25]

The president-elect, also traveling by rail, found elements of change in his journey. He arrived at Washington's Union Station thirty minutes ahead of schedule, thanks to a policy change by the Pennsylvania Railroad that permitted his train to run non-stop from Harrisburg to Baltimore, the first time that had ever happened.[26] He was met by Vice President-elect and Mrs. Coolidge, Henry Cabot Lodge, Philander Knox and other members of the Senate Committee on Arrangements, and taken by car to the Willard Hotel at 15th and Pennsylvania. After getting settled in the presidential suite, Harding and his wife were driven to the White House for a brief evening meeting with President and Mrs. Wilson. The talk was informal; the formalities could wait until the next day. The current and soon to be First Ladies had already discussed the domestic transition weeks ago. The Lincoln double bed in the Wilson's bedroom would be changed in favor of twin beds for the Hardings.[27] After tea in the Red Room, Harding and his wife returned to the Willard, attended a pre-inaugural party there and went to bed.

Friday, March 4th, was clear and cold, just as the Weather Bureau had predicted. The sky was all but cloudless, and showed signs it was losing its steel blue hue of winter. At 10:30, the Senate Committee on Arrangements and a small military honor guard escorted Harding and his entourage to the White House. There was a last informal meeting with the Wilsons, before the president, leaning on his cane and on the arm of the president-elect, shuffled outside and into a waiting Pierce Arrow automobile for the trip to Capitol Hill. Because of his condition, Wilson had to be lifted bodily into the car by his valet and his Secret Service men. He looked especially feeble alongside Harding. The wives followed in a second car; it was the first time automobiles were used to transport the principals in the inaugural ceremony.[28] Upon arriving at the Capitol, the two men were to go directly to the president's room, to allow Wilson to put the finishing touches on any remaining legislation that would mark the end of his administration. Harding made the trip on foot, while Wilson was driven to a side entrance, helped into a wheelchair, rolled up a ramp and to an elevator, and joined Harding a few minutes later.[29] When the work was done, they were joined by new and former cabinet members, as well as a Senate escort, for the brief walk to the Senate chamber to see Vice President Coolidge take his oath of office. However, Wilson would not be making the trip. His health was a matter of concern for inauguration planners, who had even provided a chair for him to use during Harding's swearing in. But the day's events had already taken its toll on his remaining energy, and he left the proceedings for his new home on the outskirts of Georgetown.[30] Once Coolidge had taken his oath and had sworn in the new members of the Senate, the group then headed for the east steps of the Capitol, where Harding would take the oath of office and deliver his address. The sparse decorations around the Capitol were complemented by the relatively small crowd that had gathered to witness the proceedings. Few of them were from out of town; the one exception was those who had traveled from Marion to see their favorite son make history. Still prime vantage points were at a premium, as tree limbs and fire hydrants were among the first spaces to be occupied. It was a small crowd by inaugural standards. The Secret Service estimated it to be no larger than fifty thousand. It was also well-behaved, partly because police were out in force to arrest anyone caught drinking and partly because a group of daredevil pilots flying in formation had captured its attention.[31] Shortly after 1:00 P.M., dignitaries began to walk down the steps to take their seats in advance of the ceremony. Wilson's attorney general, A. Mitchell Palmer, and his Navy secretary, Josephus Daniels, were among the first to arrive, followed by Senator Henry Cabot Lodge and Andrew Mellon, Harding's new treasury secretary. Secretary of State–designate Charles Evans Hughes took his seat, along with Vice President Coolidge and his predecessor, Thomas Marshall. General John Pershing and members of the Supreme Court arrived, along with Chief Justice Edward White, who would administer the oath. The crowd focused its attention on the proceedings as the Marine Band struck up a modern jazz number to coincide with Mrs. Harding's arrival. Dressed in a blue blouse and skirt, elbow-length white gloves, a diamond accented neckband, and a blue hat topped with ostrich feathers, all covered by a black fur coat, her arrival signaled the main event was soon to begin. Moments later the Marine band cut loose with "Hail to the Chief," and Warren Harding began his walk down the steps toward the kiosk. A slightly parted dark overcoat with a fur collar revealed conventional morning attire. Bareheaded, his tanned, chiseled features, dark eyebrows, and silvery hair presented a most distinguished appearance; it was a change from the tall, thin, and somewhat gaunt character who had taken the oath four years earlier. At 1:18 P.M. Warren Harding took the oath of office and became the twenty-ninth president of the United States. The Wilson years were over—yet another turn in this season of change.

Harding's inaugural address was also symbolic of the changes underway. Just thirty-seven minutes long, it was one of the shortest ever delivered by a president.[32] Although those present may have wished for his speech to copy Woodrow Wilson's crisp prose, the change in style seemed to fit the general mood of its audience. To the man on the street, the speech was precisely what he wanted to hear. It not only captured his mood but also attracted his allegiance. It was something he could support. A woman said she had heard Wilson for eight years and never understood him; she understood Harding immediately.[33]

On the whole, Harding's inaugural address left the crowd unmoved. It was an appeal for the most part for an era of good feelings, a return to normalcy, and the cultivation of home markets. Harding's words also addressed the political changes at large in the country when he dwelled for a moment on the state of women: "We want an America of homes, illuminated with hope and happiness, where mothers, freed from the necessity for long hours of toil behind their own doors, may preside as befits the hearthstone of American citizenship."[34] One of the few times the speech was interrupted by applause was his discussion of foreign affairs: "A world super-government is contrary to everything we cherish and can have no sanction by our Republic. This is not selfishness; it is sanctity. It is not aloofness; it is security. It is not suspicion of others, it is patriotic adherence to the things that made us what we are."[35] The shift in foreign policy from internationalism to modified isolation was yet another change the nation would witness and welcome. Concluding his speech with a favorite biblical passage, the Marine Band played "America the Beautiful," after which the crowd quickly dispersed and the new president retreated into the Capitol to inaugurate even more change. Since the presidency of Thomas Jefferson, presidents had customarily left the business of relaying cabinet preferences to staff members or Senate supporters. Harding revived the practice of personally appearing before the Senate to name his prospective cabinet and urge the body accelerate committee deliberations and confirm them quickly. Harding was quick to change even that, by asking the Senate to forego the usual committee deliberations and immediately confirm Senator Albert Fall as secretary of the interior. The Senate complied, and Fall became the first cabinet officer in history to be accorded such a vote of confidence.[36]

By 2:30 P.M. the business of state had been transacted for the day. The new president and his entourage exited the Capitol, climbed back into their cars, and with the military escort in the lead, were back at the White House by 2:45. The Harding years had indeed begun. There was a luncheon for family and friends followed by a brief parade. Later that day Harding issued his first presidential order, and had the gates of the White House opened, inviting passersby to stop in. He also announced plans to open certain parts of the building beginning the following week. It was yet another sign of change, in atmosphere at least, from the gloom that seemed to have hung over Washington during the Wilson war years. In the coming weeks, there would be even more change. More bulbs and flowers would be planted, and birdhouses were installed in the trees. Christmas receptions would be put back on the calendar, as were regular briefings for the White House press.

That evening, Inaugural evening, unofficial celebrations were held. Despite Harding's insistence the day be dignified and somber, there was no way to stop private observances of the change in government. Ned and Evalyn McClean sponsored a lavish bash at "Friendship," their home at 15th and I Street, just across Lafayette Square and down a block from the White House. Ned, chafing under Harding's directive as cochair of the Inaugural Committee, now cut loose, expending resources few people other than the publisher of the *Washington Post* would have at their disposal. His wife, Evalyn, helped him in this effort. She created hanging gardens with mountains of flowers on every available table, potted palm trees in every hallway, and ferns winding up every staircase. In the dining room were three 100-foot tables with goldware for several hundred guests, with creeper vines and bouquets running their length. In addition each table sported gold candelabra and white tapers.[37]

As the sun set, the guests began to arrive. It was a blend of new and old power, rising and falling stars. Alice Roosevelt and her brother Ted, the new assistant secretary of the Navy were on hand, along with Charlie Forbes, the new Veteran's Bureau chief. Attorney General Harry Daugherty showed up with companion Jess Smith, followed shortly thereafter by the new secretary of the interior, Albert Fall. Vice President and Mrs. Coolidge were there, and so were the Hardings, if only for a while. The new president was anxious to get an early start on his new job, and wanted a good night's sleep. The guest list included past and present cabinet members and Harding's former Senate colleagues, as well as anyone Harding had helped and who had returned the favor. The list was near complete, but for one notable exception. One of the architects of Harding's presidential victory was missing. As was his custom, Albert Lasker believed his job as an advertiser was to promote the product and not the promoter. He had done so with Van Camp's pork and beans and would do so with Lucky Strike cigarettes. Lasker tended to shun the spotlight when it was in his interest to do so, and tonight he wanted to be as far away from that spotlight as possible. Perhaps he sensed the shadows that would soon surround Harding and his administration. Perhaps, and more to the point, after all the time he had spent with Warren Harding, Albert Lasker could not bring himself to truly like the man he had helped elect president, or believe that Harding would be loyal to those things Lasker thought important. To work for someone he never liked or trusted was a testimony to Albert Lasker's belief that a good advertiser could sell anything to anyone, regardless of personal feelings.

NOTES

1. "Fair and Cold Weather for Inauguration Day," *New York Times*, 4 March 1921, 1.
2. Eugene P. Trani and David L. Wilson, *The Presidency of Warren G. Harding* (Lawrence: Regents Press of Kansas, 1977), 3.
3. Ibid, 6.
4. "Ready for Simple Ceremonies," *New York Times*, 4 March 1921, 1.
5. Trani, 12.
6. Ibid., 13.
7. Andrew Sinclair, *Prohibition: The Era of Excess* (Boston: Little, Brown and Company, 1962), 32.
8. Burl Noggle, *Into the Twenties: The United States from Armistice to Normalcy* (Urbana: University of Illinois Press, 1974), 158.
9. Carl Sferrazza Anthony, *Florence Harding: The First Lady, the Jazz Age, and the Death of America's Most Scandalous President* (New York: William Morrow, 1998), 205.
10. Ibid., 242.
11. "Adopt Simple Plan for Inauguration," *New York Times*, 1 March 1921, 2.
12. Ibid.
13. Francis Russell, *The Shadow of Blooming Grove: Warren G. Harding in His Times* (New York: McGraw-Hill, 1968), 437.
14. "Expect White House Dinners to Be Revived," *New York Times*, 5 March 1921, 13.
15. Anthony, 253.
16. Trani, 48.
17. John Gunther, *Taken at the Flood: The Story of Albert D. Lasker* (New York: Harper, 1960), 100. Lasker took the Shipping Board post when Herbert Hoover was named secretary of commerce.
18. Russell, 446.
19. Trani, 51.
20. Ibid., 54.
21. "All Will Be Well, Declares Harding in Marion Goodbye," *New York Times*, 3 March 1921, 1.
22. Anthony, 423.
23. "Ready for Simple Ceremonies," *New York Times*, 4 March 1921, 1.
24. "William Jennings Bryan Speech Read at Test of Inaugural Sound System," *New York Times*, 3 March 1921, 3.
25. "Airplanes Carry Times to Capital," *New York Times*, 5 March 1921, 6.
26. "Harding in Capital: Calls upon Wilson; Plans Completed for Inaugural Today,"

New York Times, 4 March 1921, 1.
   27. Russell, 424.
   28. Anthony, 259.
   29. Robert K. Murray, *The Harding Era: Warren G. Harding and His Administration* (Minneapolis: University of Minnesota Press, 1969), 110.
   30. "Harding Inaugurated: Declares against New Entanglements: Wilson, Weakened by Illness, Unable to Join in Ceremony," *New York Times,* 5 March 1921, 1.
   31. Anthony, 259.
   32. "Harding for World Court," *New York Times,* 6 March 1921, 1.
   33. Murray, 112.
   34. "Text of President Harding's Inaugural Address," *New York Times,* 5 March 1921, 5.
   35. Ibid.
   36. "Harding's New Cabinet," *New York Times,* 5 March 1921, 1; Murray, 112.
   37. Anthony, 263.

2
Albert Lasker and "Reason Why" Advertising

Albert Lasker loved to sell. As a young reporter for the Galveston, Texas, *Daily News,* he disguised himself as a Western Union messenger and sold Eugene Debs on the idea of giving him an exclusive interview. As a copy boy for the Lord & Thomas Advertising Agency, he sold his bosses on letting him have a territory vacated by another employee, and wound up producing more sales. He sold clients on the idea of letting ad agencies write as well as place copy, and on "reason why" advertising, a style that explained why one brand of product should be purchased over another. He helped sell clients on slogans such as "Keep that Schoolgirl Complexion," "The Grains Shot from Guns," and "A Cow in Every Pantry." That meant millions of dollars in sales of Palmolive Soap, Quaker Oats, and Van Camp's Evaporated Milk. He also earned millions for himself and those who followed in his footsteps. But Lasker was more than just an adman; he was an entrepreneur and a pioneer. He invested in small companies such as Pepsodent Toothpaste and used his advertising skill to grow them into corporate giants.[1] He was among the first to foresee the power of radio advertising and assembled and sponsored the first soap operas, as well as *Amos 'n' Andy*, a radio comedy.[2] He also helped sell American consumers on Kleenex tissues, Kotex sanitary napkins, Lucky Strike cigarettes, and Bob Hope.[3] He sold professional baseball on the idea of a code of ethics and an independent commissioner. He even put his money where his mouth was, taking a part ownership in the Chicago Cubs. And, finally, in 1920, he sold voters on Warren G. Harding as president of the United States. He was a man in constant motion, with his hand in many activities: politics, shipping, baseball, golf, government, show business, merchandising, public relations, aviation, civil liberties, art, philanthropy, and medical research.[4] He was also a human contradiction. A vocal Republican in his early years, he wound up a Democrat, supporting Franklin Roosevelt and Harry Truman. In foreign affairs he was an isolationist, and played an important role in keeping America out of the League of Nations after World War I. However, in later years he was an ardent supporter of the United Nations. As the president of Lord & Thomas Advertising, he resisted efforts to install a graphic arts department in his firm. He opposed any art form that distracted from the power of written advertising, yet on his own he amassed a notable collection of modern French paintings. He disliked business research, but donated millions of dollars through the Lasker Foundation to fund cancer research.[5] He was Jewish, but not terribly devout, working in an industry dominated by gentiles. Although that never proved to be an obstacle to his professional success, it occasionally influenced his personal life. When he decided to move to Lake Forest, Illinois, a wealthy suburb north of Chicago, he found himself shunned by his neighbors and barred from playing golf at the city's premier country clubs.[6] Most importantly Albert Lasker was a salesman. He had, to a commanding degree, two of the primary essentials of a good salesman: resourcefulness and a sense of fundamentals. He also had a gift of creating desires, helped in part by what many described as his unlimited powers of persuasion.

Lasker could also be sold. He began his adult life as a journalist and a Democrat but was later sold on becoming an advertiser and a Republican. Morris Lasker, his father and a successful merchant in Galveston, Texas, tolerated his son's infatuation with journalism, but wasn't enthusiastic about the career choice: "My father had a dread of my becoming a newspaper man, because in those days almost every newspaper man was a heavy drinker. I was very devoted to my father, and he proposed instead that I go to a firm that he considered a kindred field—Lord & Thomas in Chicago, an advertising agency with whom he had had some prior contact."[7]

Lord & Thomas opened its doors in 1873 at the corner of Wabash and Randolph in Chicago. Its founders, Daniel Lord and Ambrose Thomas, had both migrated from Maine to begin the venture. The agency specialized in ads for buggies, railroads, and pianos.[8] Eventually, Anheuser Busch and Armour Meat became clients. Lord & Thomas had come to Galveston to help advertise an electric trolley car company. When the business failed in the Panic of 1893, the agency stood to lose $30,000 in unpaid commissions.[9] Working through Morris Lasker, who'd been appointed to negotiate settlements for the failed concern's creditors, Lord & Thomas got what it considered to be fair treatment, and Morris Lasker got what amounted to a promise to return the courtesy if he were ever in need. In 1898 he cashed in on the favor, sending the eighteen-year old Albert to Chicago to work for Lord & Thomas for three months as a copy boy and janitor. It was to be only a trial run; at the end of ninety days Albert could return to Galveston and resume his newspaper career. But he lost all his money gambling and was forced to borrow money from Ambrose Thomas.[10] It took him over a year to repay the loan, and by that time advertising had replaced journalism as his vocation.

If Albert Lasker had some early reservations about his new line of work, he wasn't alone. As the 19th century gave way to the 20th, American businesses were themselves just beginning to come to terms with the idea of letting independent advertising agencies represent them to the public. The idea that a business would become so big it would have to depend on an outside firm to handle its advertising must have been hard to imagine. However, the march toward big business was well underway by the time independent advertising agencies arrived on the scene. The foundation, laid in stages before the Civil War, was already in place. Transportation networks, especially the railroad, were able to move people and products from one end of the United States to another. This made it possible for manufacturers to tap into a huge domestic market, thereby justifying their need for expansion. It also made industrial expansion cost effective. If the transportation system remained crude and incomplete, the costs of marketing goods in distant areas would be too high to encourage entry into those regions. Even if a manufacturer were an efficient producer, the high cost of carrying goods over considerable distances would add so much to the final price that the manufacturer could not compete with local sellers whose products traveled much shorter distances.[11]

The second half of the foundation was the revolution in communications. Business growth had chafed under the unreliable management of its affairs by mail. Some firms found that in order for their bills and invoices to reach their destinations safely, multiple copies had to be sent. Surface mail improved upon its delivery capabilities in the last quarter of the 19th century, but news of its replacement was being transmitted telegraphically. It was the rapid improvement in communications, via the telegraph, and in transportation, via the railroad, which made it possible for mass merchandisers to make the United States one large sales territory.[12] In the process the uneasy relationship between advertisers and advertising agencies was being addressed. Contracting with an advertising agency was something of a gamble. Banks often threatened to hold up business loans if word got out a firm was working with an advertising agency.[13] Most businesses simply prepared their own copy and gave it to firms such as Lord & Thomas, who in turn placed it in newspapers and magazines.

There was often deep suspicion at the corporate level that an ad agency, which didn't produce the product, could not do a better job than the producer selling it. As a result advertisers resented and frequently opposed the suggestions of the agencies, which in turn reminded their clients that ads were for the buyer's eye, not the seller's.[14] When Albert Lasker joined Lord & Thomas in 1898 (the company's 25th anniversary), it had only one copywriter, who split his days between the agency and Montgomery Ward.[15] Billings that year were $800,000, good enough for third place nationally, behind J. Walter Thompson and N. W. Ayer & Son. Unfortunately, individual accounts told the story of just how leery corporations were about buying advertising. Wrigley's Gum spent $32 on its first ad campaign; Borden's spent $513.75; Sunkist budgeted $7,500; and Procter and Gamble spent $11,543.[16] The biggest advertisers were the makers of patent medicines, who hawked their wares in inch-long, small-print ads. Some of the copy was ethical, but some of it wasn't. To make sure their products would not be hyped in similar fashion, advertisers prepared copy that did little more than describe the merchandise and tell customers where they might find it. There was no argument in favor of the product or in opposition to a competitor's. That all began to change in the early 20th century, as Albert Lasker helped transform advertising's static image into a dynamic force by using the "reason why" strategy. Acceptance of the new style came in stages, even at Lord & Thomas. First Lasker bought out Daniel Lord in 1903, and became co-owner of the agency with Ambrose Thomas.[17] Second came the appearance of John Kennedy, a copywriter who had come from Canada via Racine, Wisconsin, where he had written successful ads for a patent medicine call "Dr. Shoop's Restorative." In the spring of 1904, Kennedy landed in Lasker's Chicago office with an offer to teach him the secret of "reason why" copy writing. The theory, according to Kennedy, was that "reason why" advertising was like the salesman often found on a person's doorstep. The print version must give readers a reason why they should buy a certain product. It must be positive, but also aggressive. Lasker put Kennedy on the payroll, and together the two of them took Lord & Thomas up the ladder of the advertising hierarchy.

Two of the earliest campaigns Lasker and Kennedy collaborated on were the 1912 Ball Bearing Family Washer, and Cascarets. Copy written by another agency began with a headline: "Are You Chained to the Wash Tub?" That, said Kennedy, had a negative implication. Not everyone thought washing was a drudgery, so right away the ad had alienated potential customers. When Lord & Thomas got the account, Kennedy suggested a more positive approach. The new appeal featured the headline "Let this Machine do your Washing Free." The copy referred to the machine's motor springs, which did all the hard work, and the slats, which acted as paddles to power the washer. The ad concluded with a promise to pay the shipping and to refund the customer's money if not completely satisfied. A similar approach was used to promote the medicine Cascarets, which "don't Purge, nor Weaken nor *waste Digestive Juices* in flooding out the Bowels like Salts, Castor Oil or Cathartics. But they *act like Exercise* or [illegible] nd the Intestines, thus pushing Food on natura[illegible] Lasker became sole owner of the firm, billings [illegible] "reason why" advertising became a fixture at [illegible] be said for John Kennedy. A slow worker who [illegible] e being rushed, he eventually left the firm to t[illegible]ent. He later turned to freelancing, working fo[illegible]-profile clients such as Goodrich Tires. He ev[illegible] a brief stint, but eventually moved on.[20]

Lasker found another "reason why" disciple in Claude Hopkins. Kennedy's copy presented the unvarnished truth about a product, whereas Hopkins went in for what he called "dignified sensationalism . . . provocative statements that tickled but did not abuse the truth."[21] He came to Chicago in the early 20th century, where his attempts at "dignified sensationalism" paid off for the Swift Packing Company. Cotosuet was the company's substitute for butter and lard, made out of cottonseed oil and beef fat. It was losing its battle for market share with a rival product called Cottolene. Hopkins contacted the advertising manager of a major Chicago department store and asked if he could borrow the bay window on the 5th floor grocery department. He said he was going to put on a demonstration that would promote the store as well as Cotosuet. Next he went to a bakery and ordered a cake baked not with butter, but with Cotosuet. The cake filled the window of the grocery department, nearly touching the ceiling. According to Hopkins's estimate, over one hundred thousand people climbed four flights of stairs to see the cake. Demonstrators were there to give them samples. In addition prizes were available to anyone who could guess the overall weight of the cake, but in order to enter, every guesser had to buy a pail of Cotosuet. The stunt helped Cotosuet regain its lost market share.[22]

After touting Cotosuet for Swift, Hopkins formed a partnership with the J. L. Stack Agency, which advertised Dr. Shoop's Restorative. He used direct mail rather than newspapers to advertise the product, offering money-back guarantees to any unsatisfied customers. Liquozone was another patent medicine Claude Hopkins advertised. The product, originally produced in Canada, was bought by a Chicago businessman who spent four years trying to find someone who could successfully market it. By the time Hopkins signed on, the company was deeply in debt. Hopkins took the account in return for a share of the firm.[23] Part of Hopkins's approach was to distribute coupons to potential customers, who would then redeem them for Liquozone at local drug stores. Within a year the company showed a profit of nearly $2 million. Techniques such as money-back guarantees, coupons, and free samples were quickly becoming Hopkins's trademarks, but it was his work for Schlitz Beer that caused Hopkins to surface on Lasker's radar and made him an essential weapon in Lord & Thomas's advertising arsenal. Schlitz, another J. L. Stack client and the fifth-largest brewer in the United States, was looking for a way to increase market share. The current campaign simply touting the beer's purity was sputtering because other brewers were doing the same. Hopkins concluded that these unsubstantiated claims would not get the job done. Beer drinkers needed to be told why Schlitz beer was better than the rest. Hopkins went to brewing school and then toured the Schlitz brewery, where he witnessed firsthand the purification process: " I saw rooms where beer was dripping over pipes, so the beer could be cooled in purity. They cleaned every pump and pipe twice daily to avoid contamination. Every bottle was cleaned four times by machinery. I said: Why don't you tell people these things? Why do you merely cry your been is pure? Why don't you tell them the reasons?"[24] Even though every brewery went through the same purification process, none had bothered to tell beer drinkers about it. What if Hopkins advertised Schlitz's brewing techniques in a way that implied it was doing something more complicated and expensive than its competitors, but wasn't charging extra for it? No other brewery would be able to make a similar claim without sounding like a Schlitz copycat.

The campaign was a roaring success, and sent Schlitz into a first-place tie with Anheuser Busch, which also happened to be a Lasker client. In one of Hopkins's ads, "Poor Beer vs. Pure Beer," he compared Schlitz to others, listing all the purification techniques he had seen, and underlined the fact that all this work was being done at no extra cost to the consumer. The approach caught the eye of Cyrus Curtis, founder of the Curtis Publishing Company, which owned *The Saturday Evening Post* and the *Ladies' Home Journal*. Curtis was on a train to Philadelphia, and while headed for the dining car, he bumped into Lasker. Curtis had banned alcohol ads from his publications and had never, as far as anyone knew, taken a drink. But that was about to change: "Lasker," he said, "I am about to order a bottle of Schlitz Beer as a result of an advertisement I just read, and you ought to go out and get the man who wrote that advertisement."[25]

Returning to Chicago, Lasker found Hopkins and convinced him to join Lord & Thomas. It would prove to be an effective, albeit strange, alliance. Hopkins was the mild-mannered son of a newspaper publisher and a schoolteacher, and had experienced a precarious financial existence as a child. Lasker, on the other hand, had grown up in wealth and was no shrinking violet. Neither went to college, a fact Hopkins partially credited for his success: "I know nothing of value that an advertising man can be taught in college. I know of many things taught there that he will need to un-learn before he can steer any practical course."[26] They were also very hard workers for whom normal hours meant nothing. Hopkins could put together an entire year's advertising campaign in a matter of days. They also shared the same idea of advertising's purpose: the creation of both profit and demand for products.[27] Among the products Lasker and Hopkins created a demand for were those items considered unknown, unpopular, or socially unacceptable, including Quaker Oats, Kotex sanitary napkins and Lucky Strike cigarettes.

Up until 1909 Quaker Oats advertised their two leading breakfast foods, Wheat Berries and Puffed Rice, through an advertising agency it owned. The budget was small and so were sales when compared with Post and Kellogg: "In the advertising for 'Puffed Rice,' they showed Japanese people and had Japanese figures. They showed the rice was large and they said that it was very delicious. There was very little argument, just a few words. I do not even believe they showed the goods. The 'Wheat Berries' they advertised as a delicious new wheat food was enlarged. There was no story, no argument. They merely offered the merchandise."[28] Lord & Thomas won the account and got to work.

It was during a tour of Quaker's manufacturing facility in Iowa that Claude Hopkins found the strategy that would change Wheat Berries to Puffed Wheat, and Quaker Oats from a novelty to a mainstay in the breakfast food world. The factory in Davenport featured a two- to three-story room with a platform. Inside, workers had built what looked very much like a wooden gun, into which they put the wheat or rice. The mouth of the gun was covered and heated to a high temperature. At a certain point the cover was lifted, and the rice or wheat, now eight times its original size, flew out of the gun and landed all over the floor.[29]

Hopkins, armed with what he had seen on his Iowa tour, returned to Chicago and prepared an ad campaign for Quaker: "Puffed Wheat and Puffed Rice, the Food Shot from Guns." The advertising showed pictures or drawings of the guns firing the grains to the ceiling of the plant. Within six weeks sales of both products had increased.[30]

The campaign to make Kotex a household word was launched in 1921. The Kimberly Clark Corporation had responded to the World War I shortage of cotton for use in bandages and surgical supplies by creating "cellucotton," a cellulose by-product.[31] Cellucotton filled not only that need but also an unexpected one. During the war nurses began using the product for sanitary napkins, and later Kotex (short for cotton-line texture) was put on the market. The product failed miserably in the early going, victimized in part by such vague advertising that few consumers understood what it was. It was also stymied by the general consensus that public discussion of menstruation was in poor taste. Lord & Thomas landed the account in 1926.[32] The new campaign featured not only clever "reason why" advertising but also clever marketing and public relations. Lasker organized a campaign to inform school boards and other organizations all over the country about Kotex, and how teachers could perform a valuable public service by instructing girl students about feminine hygiene.[33] Then he persuaded the *Ladies' Home Journal* to publish an article about menstruation (it eventually ran ads for the product). Finally he engineered a way to make the sale of sanitary napkins a less embarrassing experience for women. Newspaper advertisements told them that Kotex, in a plain, wrapped package that gave no clue to its identity, would be available in shops and didn't even have to be asked for by name. The customer could put fifty cents in a box near a pile of packages, take one, and walk out without having to say a word.[34]

One of the most important accounts Lord & Thomas ever handled was the American Tobacco Company, and, in particular, Lucky Strike cigarettes. By the end of the 1920s, the account represented 58 percent of the agency's billings.[35] Life in the United States after World War I had undergone many changes, but tobacco consumption among men remained still pretty much the way it was before. Men either chewed tobacco or smoked cigars or pipes. However, as the popularity of manufactured cigarettes grew, tobacco companies began experimenting with different blends, such as Virginia and Turkish tobaccos. Camels, produced by Reynolds, and Chesterfields, produced by Liggett & Myers, featured those blends, making them pioneers in the field, as well as overall sales leaders. Lucky Strike was well back in the pack and was in danger of being snuffed out by the competition, which totaled more than fifty types of cigarettes, cigars, pipe, and chewing tobaccos.

One of the first things Albert Lasker did after landing the account in 1923 was to redirect its approach to include a long-excluded segment of the consuming population: women. Women were not allowed to smoke, at least in public, so when the urge to light up struck them, especially when dining out, they often had to seek refuge in the ladies restroom.[36] Making it socially acceptable for women to smoke in public would double sales for everyone, including Lucky Strike, but changing public attitudes was going to be tricky. However, a pivotal event that may have prompted Lasker to take up the challenge, happened in Chicago and involved him and his first wife. On the advice of her doctor, Flora Lasker had taken up smoking as a way to curb her appetite. When she lit up in the main dining room of Chicago's Tip Top Inn, the owner told her that she and Albert would have to move to a private dining room in deference to patrons who were objecting. "It filled me with indignation that I had to do surreptitiously something which was perfectly normal in a place where I had gone so much. That determined me to break down the prejudice against women smoking. I think this campaign was one of the few we put under my direction at Lord & Thomas, and that was largely my own idea."[37] The issue had become personal for Lasker, and he used his clout with Lucky Strike to redress that personal grievance and recalibrate social customs.

The advertising campaign evolved in two stages. First Lasker would have to create an environment where women could feel comfortable about smoking in public. Society as a whole was not going to grant that automatically. Therefore women would have to convince other women that it was okay. The women who would promote the idea would have to be secure in their positions, unassailable, and insulated from any possible backlash. Lasker concluded that European women, especially those in the performing arts, might be the answer. Many social taboos had already fallen in Europe, and Lasker thought these women might be worthy of emulation by their American counterparts. He convinced a group of celebrated singers to give testimonials for Lucky Strike as part of its "Precious Voice" campaign: "As they were singers, they said, 'My living is dependent on my being able to sing, and I protect my precious voice by smoking Lucky Strike.' The campaign was a very alluring one, because it was built around alluring people. It was very dramatic in that they testified that . . . by smoking Lucky Strike . . . there would be no rasp and no ill consequences."[38] Other ads proclaimed, "Cigarettes Are Kind To Your Throat." Before long a number of artists with the Metropolitan Opera of New York had provided testimonials, lending their credibility and their voices in return for national publicity.[39] The power of the testimonial, which was nothing new in advertising, was now linked with the power of "reason why" advertising and began to reshape the advertising world. Coaches and athletes also recommended Luckies for throat protection, but the main focus continued to be women.

The second part of the Lucky Strike ad campaign was more defensive in nature. If women were to turn to smoking as a way to maintain their health, or in Flora Lasker's case, to control her weight, confectioners could hardly be expected to do nothing in response. Meeting in Pittsburgh, they planned to respond with an advertising campaign of their own. "Their main argument that they were going to put forward was that cigarette smoking was not good for the nervous system and for general health. The way to stop it (smoking) was to eat a piece of candy. If you ate a piece of candy, the sweetness of that would fix your saliva so that you would lose your taste to smoke. Then I remembered that the doctor had told my wife to smoke to cut down on her appetite. That justified us in reverse in making the claim for Lucky Strike."[40]

Lasker and the American Tobacco Company fought back, spending millions of dollars to drown out the candy industry. Ads bombarded women, warning them that candy contributed to obesity. Smoking could reduce candy cravings, thus cutting down on those unflattering calories. "Then we added to our copy with each of our testifiers that they protected their precious voices by smoking Luckies, and that they protected their figures by 'reaching for a Lucky instead of a sweet.'"[41] "Reach For a Lucky Instead of a Sweet," urged the copy, and figure-conscious women, influenced by medical reassurances and feminine celebrities, put down the candy and lit up. The impact of the campaign was awesome. Within a year of taking the account, Lasker and Lord & Thomas had increased sales by 312 percent. Accordingly, Lucky Strike's advertising budget went from $400,000 in 1925 to $19 million in 1931.[42]

Perhaps one of the most significant campaigns undertaken by Albert Lasker was his work for the Van Camp's Corporation. It was important for several reasons. First it was an Indiana corporation seeking to snag national sales. Second purchasing canned foods was a new idea for American consumers. To sell canned foods, in this case pork and beans (and later canned milk), would require a shift in consumer habits. Finally the contacts Albert Lasker made during this campaign would gradually steer him toward the national political arena.

The immediate job at hand, selling canned pork and beans, would require the best of Lord & Thomas's research skills and the copy writing and creativity that

Lasker could produce. Market research revealed that only a fraction of American housewives bought canned pork and beans; the rest made them at home. It was a time-consuming process that rarely produced a satisfactory product. Lasker saw his opportunity and exploited it. He wrote ads talking about "A 16 Hour Job": "Home-baked beans, with the soaking, boiling and baking are a slow, costly dish to prepare. Then, some beans are crisped and some broken, some are hard and some mushy. The skins are tough. Much flavor has escaped. And the beans are always hard to digest." Lasker's approach was not to undercut another company's product—at least not yet. First he had to convince women that the dish they were preparing in the home was inferior to the product Van Camp's was offering. His message had to have balance: hardheaded "reason why" advertising coupled with a gentle prod to women that switching to store-bought pork and beans would save them time and give their family the best nutrition. Other ads mentioned that Van Camp's Pork and Beans were "A Studied Dish": "We select the beans. Our boiling water is free of minerals. Hard water makes the skins tough. Van Camp's are baked in modern steam ovens. This baking makes beans easy to digest. Van Camp's are baked under scientific cooks. They have spent years perfecting this delicious, hygienic dish." Careful not to alienate women whose business he wanted, Lasker's ads promoted the freedom women would enjoy with this product, and the wonderful benefits waiting for their family inside every can of Van Camp's Pork and Beans. Ads promoting Van Camp's were inserted in publications such as the *Ladies' Home Journal,* but for the campaign to be successful, men also had to be sold and Van Camp's had to be separated from the growing field of pork and beans producers. To win the men's vote, Lasker initiated test and *taste* marketing. Lord & Thomas sent observers into downtown Indianapolis, where they staked out restaurants and lunch counters, trying to find out what men ate for the noonday meals. Surprisingly the dish of choice was pork and beans. The observers returned to the restaurants armed with complimentary cans of Van Camp's Pork and Beans. The printed appeal to men appeared in the *Saturday Evening Post,* where they were encouraged to ask waiters at their favorite restaurants to "Tell Me the Secret of These Pork and Beans": "He will, if he likes you, probably tell you the truth. He may bring you in an empty can of Van Camp's, bring it wrapped in a napkin to show you the brand. This is the secret of superlative Baked Beans, at home or anywhere." Lasker used his copywriting skills to conclude that because men seemed to like pork and beans for lunch, and because Van Camp's was supplying canned pork and beans to restaurants across town, wouldn't it make sense for women to serve Van Camp's at home?

Finally in an attempt to distance Van Camp's from the rest of the competition, Lord & Thomas arranged for a demonstration lunch, where Van Camp's and other pork and beans were served to a jury. Consumers not taking part in the lunch were urged in advertisements to try van Camp's rivals so they too could see the difference. The dare paid off. People assumed that Van Camp's must be pretty good if they felt confident enough to pit its product dish to dish against the competition. Just like an earlier invitation to beer drinkers to visit the Schlitz brewery to see the purification process firsthand, the decision to invite consumers to sample other pork and beans before settling on Van Camp's was another example of Lasker's use of "reason why" advertising. It gave the public hardheaded, logical reasons why one product should be purchased over another.

The Van Camp's episode began Albert Lasker's journey into national politics. While working for Van Camp's, Lasker met William Irwin, an Indiana banker, who later became that state's Republican National Committeeman.[43] Irwin's assessment of Lasker's advertising skills was passed on to the Republican Party, and in 1918, another Hoosier, Will Hays, the newly elected chairman of the Republican National Committee, reached out for Lasker as the GOP began its quest for control of Congress and the White House.[44]

NOTES

1. "Exit the Old Master," *Time,* 9 June 1952, 94–96.
2. "Prince of Hucksters," *Time,* 29 August 1960, 68–70.
3. Ibid.
4. John Gunther, *Taken at the Flood: The Story of Albert D. Lasker* (New York: Harper, 1960), 4.
5. Ibid., 6
6. Ibid., 80. Lasker solved his golfing problem by building an eighteen-hole golf course on his 400-acre Lake Forest estate. It was, at the time, the largest private golf course west of New York.
7. "The Personal Reminiscences of Albert Lasker," conducted by the Columbia University Oral History Research Office, 1948–1950, 7 (hereafter cited as Lasker).
8. Foote, Cone & Belding Register of Lord & Thomas Advertising files on deposit at the Wisconsin State Historical Society's Mass Communications Division (hereafter cited as FCBR).
9. Lasker, 9.
10. Ibid., 11.
11. Glenn Porter, *The Rise of Big Business* (Wheeling, Ill.: Harlan Davidson, Inc., 1992), 42.
12. Ibid., 44.
13. Lasker, 20.
14. Pamela Laird, *Advertising Progress: American Business and the Rise of Consumer Marketing* (Baltimore: Johns Hopkins University Press, 1998), 198.
15. Lasker, 16.
16. Gunther, 42.
17. Lasker, 45. Lasker's rise was impressive, given the fact he had started at the firm in 1898 as a copy boy and janitor, earning $10 a week.
18. Gunther, 179.
19. Stephen R. Fox, *The Mirror Makers: A History of American Advertising and Its Creators* (New York: William Morrow, 1984), 61.
20. Ibid., 51.
21. Claude C. Hopkins, *Scientific Advertising* (Chicago: Advertising Publications [reprint], 1966), 54.
22. Claude C. Hopkins, *My Life in Advertising* (Chicago: Advertising Publications [reprint], 1966), 108. Students of Chicago history will take note that Hopkins contacted the Rothchild Department Store regarding use of the bakery window and ordered the cake from Kohlstaat's Bakery, which had a store nearby.
23. Hopkins, *Scientific Advertising,* 93.
24. Ibid., 84.

25. Gunther, 68.
26. Hopkins, *My Life in Advertising,* 9.
27. Lasker, 55. Lasker once said that because Hopkins worked so fast, he sometimes had to delay client presentations for weeks because he was sure they wouldn't believe that enough time had been put into it.
28. Lasker, 58.
29. Arthur F. Marquette, *Brands, Trademarks and Good Will: The Story of the Quaker Oats Company* (New York: McGraw-Hill, 1967), 103.
30. Lasker, 62. Sales increased despite the fact prices for both products were increased. Lasker told Quaker the current margin seemed too small to educate the public, "for the public must always pay for its education."
31. Gunther, 154.
32. FCBR, 26.
33. Gunther, 154. Lasker was now without the services of Claude Hopkins, who retired for good in 1924.
34. Ibid.
35. Ibid., 163.
36. Lasker, 106.
37. Ibid., 108. The Tip Top Inn was in the Pullman Building, at the corner of Michigan and Adams. During its heyday it was a gathering place for entertainers, including George M. Cohan and Anna Held. The Pullman Building also featured a number of luxury apartments, one of which was occupied by showman Florenz Ziegfeld. The building was demolished in 1956.
38. Ibid., 109–110.
39. Ibid., 110.
40. Ibid., 111.
41. Ibid., 113.
42. Gunther, 169.
43. Lasker, 55.
44. Ibid.

3
Pork, Beans, and Politics

The use of advertising in American presidential politics probably goes back at least as far as the American presidency itself. As America changed from a rural agrarian society to an urban industrialized one, the methods of promoting presidential candidates did likewise. Handbills, posters, pamphlets, and campaign songs, not to mention other tools, have all played a role. Presidential advertising's growth and importance spread through the 19th century, but it really wasn't until the beginning of the 20th century that advertisers, taking advantage of new communications technologies, began to have a major impact on presidential politics. Photography and motion pictures mutually provided candidates and voters with a degree of access and immediacy that had not been experienced except in face-to-face situations.

Most scholars writing on the topic of modern advertising and politics have tended to devote a majority of their time to the efforts of George Creel and Bruce Barton. Creel led the Committee on Public Information during World War I and helped to win public support for the conflict, and Barton advised the Republican Party. Both men have been recognized as symbols of advertising's new potential as a tool to educate consumers and sensitize producers about consumer needs. Barton told Republican leaders that the 1924 presidential election should feature efforts to portray the nominee as a warm human being who would touch the emotions of the American people.[1] Calvin Coolidge would come to play Eliza Doolittle to Barton's Henry Higgins, the end result being a Republican victory.

Bruce Barton may have been an important political humanizer, but he wasn't the first. Albert Lasker sold voters on Warren Harding in 1920 the same way Barton proposed to sell Coolidge—by creating a warm, friendly image of someone most voters could relate to. Perhaps Barton should get credit for doing more with less, but that's an entirely different story.

However, the Harding campaign wasn't Albert Lasker's first foray into the political arena. That happened twenty-five years earlier in Texas. Lasker had shared reporting duties on the *Galveston Daily News* with a man who also moonlighted for Populist William Jennings Bryan. When Bryan won the Democratic presidential nomination in 1896, he hired the man as his press secretary. Campaign reporting then became Lasker's primary beat, and he was assigned to cover R. B. Hawley's congressional campaign. Lasker traveled with Hawley, reporting back to the paper and occasionally acting as Hawley's secretary. "I helped Mr. Hawley with his speeches. I had to study the Republican campaign textbooks and get matter out of the textbooks for him. I convinced myself, and became a Republican. Mr. Hawley was elected and may have been the first Republican congressman to represent the South since the end of the Civil War."[2]

But it was pork and beans that really got Lasker involved in national politics. His advertising of Van Camp's Pork and Beans helped make the company a hit with housewives across the country. Lasker himself was so sure of the product that he advanced the company a year of free advertising. When the owners couldn't make good on the bill, they did the next best thing and gave Lasker and four other large creditors a stake in the company: "One of these four men was William G. Irwin from Columbus, Indiana, who was one of the most influential industrialists and financiers in the state. He subsequently became Republican National Committeeman from Indiana."[3]

Irwin became Indiana's Republican National Committeeman in 1918, the same year fellow Hoosier Will H. Hays was elected RNC chairman.[4] The young Indianapolis attorney had caught the eye of national Republican leaders and may have been one of the few bright spots in an otherwise dismal record turned in by the GOP dating back to 1907. As the Progressive movement gained support within the Republican Party, an internal struggle began to brew between party insurgents and the old guard. The tone of the debate sharpened between 1909 and 1912 as President William Howard Taft sparred with his predecessor and mentor Theodore Roosevelt. In 1910 Democrats capitalized on the rift and captured control of the House of Representatives. Two years later Roosevelt openly broke with Old Guard Republicans and challenged Taft's renomination. The intraparty bloodletting helped the Democratic Party elect Woodrow Wilson president and take over the Senate. The GOP enjoyed a partial recovery in 1914, thanks in part to a soft economy and a partial truce with Progressives. The congressional elections that year gave it enough momentum to think Wilson could be beaten in 1916.[5]

The presidential election that year was close. Wilson and the nation had to wait three days to find out if he'd been reelected. In the end, California was the deciding factor. A razor thin plurality gave him the state and its all-important electoral votes.[6] However, the news wasn't all bad for the GOP. It had pulled even with Democrats in the House, where each party now controlled 215 seats. In the Senate the Democratic majority had been trimmed to just twelve. The legislative returns were an indication of how short Wilson's coattails were, and how close the Republicans were to being back in charge. The White House might have been home to Republican presidential nominee Charles Evans Hughes if things had gone differently in California. Hughes had reached out to Progressives, even including them in his national organization, but Old Guard Republicans, still angry about the intraparty strife back in 1912, seized every possible opportunity to exclude Progressives from the campaign. The ultimate snub occurred in California, where Hughes stumped the state but refused to meet with Senate candidate and key Progressive Hiram Johnson. Had these slights not been dealt California's Progressives, and had the GOP done a better job of fine tuning its message and getting it to the right voters, things might have been different.[7]

Enter Will Hays. Elected chairman of the Indiana GOP in 1914, he had helped to heal the rift between Republicans and Progressives, and his methods had been viewed as a possible formula for national reconciliation. He brought Progressives into the state GOP's hierarchy. He also kept the party active year-round, especially in nonelection years. He developed schools to train county chairmen and committeemen. He recruited an army of speakers who fanned out across the state bearing a unified Republican message. His election as national chairman marked a further triumph for national conciliation and put into authority a man who practiced party unity: "The Republican National Committee decided it was time to bring in as chairman a man who had never been in national politics, and therefore not connected with any faction. . . . They elected Will Hays."[8]

Hays spent the first few months as chairman traveling the country in order to rebuild the party and shore up his support. He spent a considerable amount of time in New York, Ohio, and especially California, where he brokered a truce between Republicans and Progressives.[9] However, within the party debate continued to rage on a number of issues, including World War I and American participation in postwar international affairs. That debate intensified in January 1918 when Woodrow Wilson unveiled his Fourteen Points, which included his plan for a League of Nations. Almost immediately, factions began to form within the GOP regarding the League. Theodore Roosevelt and Hiram Johnson led the isolationist camp, whereas Massachusetts Senator Henry Cabot Lodge and his supporters called for revisions of Wilson's plan.[10] A third group led by former President Taft felt some type of international coalition was worth considering. The potential for another messy, rancorous, and divisive intraparty feud seemed great. If trying to put out that fire wasn't enough, Hays also found himself in charge of a political party that was badly in need of cash. He contacted Will Irwin, Indiana's Republican National Committeeman, for advice. Irwin recalled his Van Camp's association with Lasker, and how Lasker had given the company a generous line of credit while advertising its products. Lasker could help the party with its cash-flow problems as well as its image. Irwin wrote Hays a letter of introduction. Lasker, intrigued by the request for the meeting, received Hays when he came to Chicago. Lasker wanted some kind of war-related job, but Hays was interested only in enlisting him in the Republican Party. Lasker had made sick businesses well; Hays hoped Lasker could do the same for the GOP. Lasker, however, wasn't ready to commit on the strength of Hays's appeal, so the young RNC chairman closed the deal by sending Lasker to confer with Teddy Roosevelt, whom the ad man idolized. "There were several steps leading up to the porch (of Roosevelt's Oyster Bay, New York, home) and Colonel Roosevelt was standing at the top. When I came up, without any introduction, he put his arm around me and said, 'So this is Lasker. They tell me you're the greatest advertiser in America.' I remember my reply: 'In your presence, Colonel, who would have the temerity to claim that distinction?'"[11] Roosevelt followed Hays's lead and steered Lasker into working for the Republican National Committee. Lasker was sold on the idea when Roosevelt warned him that Wilson's activities could drag the United States into permanent European entanglements.[12] Lasker, whose mother and father had fled Germany in the 1850s to escape a system that was "grinding down individualism," was convinced that "America could only help Europe by staying independent." He agreed to help Hays and the RNC in whatever way he could.[13]

The GOP faced a number of problems as the 1918 congressional elections approached. First and foremost was the continuing, isolationist-internationalist debate that threatened to destroy the reconciliation process. Without unity, the party would never be able to muster a voter turnout sufficient enough to regain control of Congress. One of Lasker's first tasks as assistant RNC chairman in charge of publicity was to find some common ground on which Republicans could unite against the Democrats. He was also supposed to be helping out with the GOP's cash-flow problems; it was rapidly becoming a job easier said than done. Because of the party's internal problems and their failures at the polls, most investors rejected RNC solicitation efforts. Without money it would be near impossible to get the Republicans' message to voters. Will Hays met with Reed Smoot, chairman of the Republican Senatorial Campaign Committee, and Simeon Fess, who handled GOP campaign activities for the House of Representatives. Both men agreed that at least $300,000 would be needed in order to finance a well-run congressional campaign.[14] Hays had no idea where the money was going to come from; even Lasker didn't have that much to spend at the time. The answer to the GOP's funding problems appeared before Hays while he attended a New York luncheon in February 1918. William Boyce Thompson was an Arizona industrialist who'd made a fortune in copper mining. He offered to do whatever he could to help the Republican Party. Hays told him what he needed, and Thompson and a few of his associates underwrote the campaign.[15]

With the money problem temporarily under control, the Republican leaders could now focus on finding an issue that would galvanize the party into unified action. Instead the issue found them. In the fall of 1918, Wilson reversed his wartime nonpartisan "politics is adjourned" stance in favor of a very partisan push for a Democrat-controlled Congress. He figured a like-minded legislative branch would strengthen his position when dealing with European leaders after the war and would facilitate his campaign for the Fourteen Points at home. Wilson went public with his appeal in October: "If you have approved of my leadership and wish me to continue to be your unembarrassed spokesman in affairs at home and abroad, I earnestly beg that you will express yourselves unmistakably to that effect by returning a Democratic majority to both the Senate and House of Representatives."[16] He claimed that while Republicans had been pro-war, they had also been antiadministration and were proving harmful to the war effort. He warned that a Republican majority in Congress would undermine him, making postwar dealings with America's European allies, as well as Germany, difficult. He asked voters to act not for his sake, or for the sake of a political party, but for the sake of the country.

There's no telling what impact Wilson's appeal may have had on voters had it

Pork, Beans, and Politics

not been seized upon by Repu[...] [...]olden opportunity. If the president's comme[...] [...]a threat to the democratic process, then the G[...] [...]ress. Hays and Lasker went to work. An RNC [...] [...]established on the third floor of New York Cit[...] [...]t corner of 5th Avenue and 40th Street.[17] A tw[...] [...]of authors and writers who had volunteered th[...] [...]ker's supervision.[18]

The RNC's eleventh hour push to unite Republicans and regain control of Congress began on October 28 with a blistering attack on Wilson's partisan appeal. The message bore many of the "reason why" advertising tactics Lasker used when he was working with commercial clients at Lord & Thomas. In a statement to Republicans across the country, Will Hays claimed "the President has questioned the motives and fidelity of your representatives in Congress. He has thereby impugned their loyalty and denied their patriotism. His challenge is to you who elected those representatives. You owe it to them, to the honor of your great party and to your own self respect to meet that challenge squarely, not only as Republicans, but as Americans."[19] According to Hays, the President had cast a slur on Republican patriotism and was 'ungracious . . . wanton . . . mendacious.'"[20] His comments as to why Republicans should repudiate Wilson at the polls the following week contained more of Lasker's "reason why" advertising logic: "Republicans have been pro-war. Then why does he [Wilson] demand their defeat? It is because they are for peace through, not without, victory; because they do not believe lasting peace can be obtained through negotiation; because they consider that 'U.S.' stands for 'Unconditional Surrender' as well as for the United States and Uncle Sam. Mr. Wilson does not. The Democratic Congress does not. There is the issue as clear as the noonday sun."[21]

Lasker, through Will Hays, had compared Republicans with Democrats, just as he had compared Van Camp's Pork and Beans with homemade. He had couched his argument within the claim that Republican patriotism had been demeaned and the fear that Wilson was out to do damage to the Constitution: "He [Wilson] calls for the defeat of pro-war Republicans and the election of anti-war Democrats. He, as the Executive, is no longer satisfied to be one branch of the Government, as provided by the Constitution. Republican Congressmen must be defeated, and the Democratic Congressmen must, as they would, yield in everything. That is evidently his idea—the idea of an autocrat calling himself the servant, but bidding for the mastery of this great, free people."[22]

The whole tone of the Republican attack characterized the President as someone ungrateful for the contributions and sacrifices made by Republicans and their elected officials, and created an image of him as a power-hungry executive intent on depriving the people of their political rights. If played properly it could have the effect of galvanizing Republicans, be they Progressive or Old Guard, into dropping their differences and joining forces against a common foe. But in order to close the rift, at least in time for the November elections, something else would be needed. A public gesture, dignified, yet still sensational, by two of the more prominent players in the Republican Party, each representing different points of view, might do the trick. They would have to avoid specifics, for fear of unintentionally hurting the cause. Whatever they said would have to continue to focus public scrutiny on Wilson and the Democratic Party. The players turned out to be none other than Theodore Roosevelt and William Howard Taft, former friends and former presidents. Their pubic reconciliation, in the name of party unity, was effective, especially coming less than a week before the November elections. They urged "all Americans who are Americans first to vote for a Republican Congress."[23] The two men included in the appeal their concern about the current president's intentions. They claimed that "a Republican Congress is needed as a check upon one-man power in the making of peace treaties, and in the work of reconstruction that must follow the war, as well as on the ground that somebody vested with constitutional powers and not under the domination of President Wilson to demand an accounting from the present Administration in Washington of its war stewardship."[24] The stunt, in both format and context, was something Lasker excelled at: dignified, yet sensational. It would be a tactic he would return to time and again during his service with the Republican Party.

Wilson's political blunder, and the GOP's ability to use it as a way to unite itself and mobilize public opinion, seemed to be working. Reports filtering into party headquarters in New York prompted Hays to announce that "the Republican Party will carry both the House and the Senate. To equal the democratic vote in the Senate, the Republicans need to gain only four votes. We will gain at least seven. To equal the Democratic vote in the House the Republicans need to gain only five votes. We will gain at least twenty-six."[25]

At RNC headquarters in Washington, GOP officials were evaluating Hays's projections as akin to whistling past the graveyard. Their concerns were enough to prompt Hays to publicize an appeal by William Howard Taft to Ohio Republicans. Taft called upon the state to "redeem herself from the mistakes she made two years ago. . . . I sincerely hope that Republicans of Ohio will stand united for state and congressional tickets. The issue made by the President's appeal is one that should bind all Republicans without regard to personal considerations. The issue whether we shall yield to one-man power to meet the great problems of the next two years should be met by all loyal Republicans with an answer that can leave no doubt."[26]

That Tuesday, November 5, Republicans rolled to their largest electoral plurality since 1906, getting 1.2 million more votes than the Democrats.[27] The Republican Party now controlled the Senate by a 49–47 margin, and the House by a 239–194 spread. The results weren't exactly what Hays had predicted, but no one seemed to be complaining. The victory gave the GOP control of all committee chairmanships and marked the party's apparent reunion and revival after the years of division and defeat that had set in at the end of Theodore Roosevelt's second term as president.

If success is said to have a thousand fathers but failure is an orphan, then the Republican Party's success in 1918 should be a case of happy yet confusing paternity. Many forces were responsible beyond Wilson's partisan appeal. Northern and western farmers, who had supported the Democrats in 1916, abandoned them in 1918, convinced southern farmers were getting preferential pricing policies from Congress split the Democratic alliance.²⁹ [...] their own cause by mending fe[...] on issues of peace and war pro[...] the future seemed to indicate a[...] presidential victory in 1920.

[...]tholicism also [...]ans had helped [...]en the factions [...]ent, nothing in [...]nent unity and

Woodrow Wilson's October n[...]ment that helped accelerate th[...] beyond intraparty differences a[...] [...] It was his com[...] licans to look [...] the big picture. To that end, then, credit must be given the Republican National Committee and the publicity team it assembled under Albert Lasker. He used the president's appeal as a way to refocus Republican and voter interest in the campaign. His application of "reason why" advertising techniques, comparing Wilson's desire for a compliant Congress as being undemocratic and stressing the GOP's dedication to constitutionality, may have been the "salesmanship in print" that helped turn the tide—and the tables. Democrats were now being perceived as the party that took the nation to war to save world democracy, and was apparently willing to sacrifice American democracy in the process. Lasker helped the GOP stake out its position as guarantors of familiar American customs and practices, and the Democratic Party found itself unable to recover in 1918 or in 1920.

Lasker's experiences and the Republican Party's success in 1918 gave the advertising executive a measure of clout he intended to use. He wanted to educate the GOP about a number of issues still dividing the party and important to Lasker himself. One of them was the possible U.S. participation in the League of Nations. He had grown up in a household concerned that the United States must avoid European entanglements.³⁰ Despite the congressional successes of 1918, the party was still divided on the League issue. As the head of a major advertising agency, as well as RNC assistant chairman in charge of publicity, Lasker found himself at the right place, at the right time, and with the right tools to warn the GOP what might happen if Wilson's vision of the postwar world became a reality. "I was working for Mr. Hays when an American living in Paris called upon us. I spent several hours with this man; he opened my eyes to the fact that Wilson was working toward what subsequently became the League of Nations. . . . It was not a good thing for the United States. I had this man write some pamphlets. As I remember, one of the pamphlets was entitled, *After the Peace, What?* I paid the cost of printing copies of this pamphlet and distributing it among party workers. Mr. Hays had no funds with which to print and distribute them. I did this on my own, of course receiving Mr. Hays' permission to proceed."³¹

Hays may have given his blessing to the project, but that was all he could afford to do. The RNC was still living off the payments being channeled to it by Arizona mining tycoon William Boyce Thompson. The party remained in dire need of money as well as grassroots support between 1918 and 1920. Hays tried to solve both problems early in 1918 when he announced the Republican Party would not accept individual contributions of more than $1,000.³² The announcement seemed to foster the perception that the GOP was reaching out to modest donors in order to broaden its base of popular support. However, in 1918, donors such as Chicago meat packer Ogden Armour, who gave $5,000, and San Francisco banker Will Crocker, who gave $3,000, hardly fell into that category.[33] Still the public announcement captured the moral high ground on the issue for Republicans, a form of preemptive advertising that would later cast the Democratic Party in an unfavorable light when it tried to make the same appeal.

Lasker's donations of money, time, and expertise to the Republican Party in the 1918 congressional elections helped to increase his visibility and his influence in policy issues. He used that influence to continue to warn about the dangers of American participation in any kind of postwar arrangement, especially anything engineered by Woodrow Wilson. The pamphlet he had published was one of his first attempts to create consensus within the GOP regarding the League of Nations. In 1919 he complained to Hays that he thought senators waging the congressional battle against the League were not making satisfactory headway. Based on Lasker's concerns, Hays arranged what must have been an extraordinary dinner meeting at the Shoreham Hotel in Washington, D.C. Summoned to explain their progress to Lasker were Henry Cabot Lodge (Massachusetts), chairman of the Senate Foreign Relations Committee, and fellow Senators Frank Brandegee (Connecticut) and Medill McCormick (Illinois). They listened as Lasker, speaking on behalf of a number of influential party members presented their concerns. Then Lodge took to the floor and "traced with fine logic what the Senate had been doing. He said 'I want the progress to be faster, just as you do, but there are only fourteen of us [on the Foreign Relations Committee], and we've got to bring along a lot more if we are to have the necessary one-third vote to defeat the League proposal. Remember; a general who gets ahead of his army loses the battle. I can't go any faster than I can get my army to follow.'"[34] Although Lasker left the meeting somewhat reassured as to the efforts being made in opposition to the League, he also left convinced the Republican Party had not reached consensus on the issue. It would become the principal mission of the king of "reason why" advertising to correct that by November 1920.

NOTES

1. Philip Gold, *Advertising, Politics, and American Culture: From Salesmanship to Therapy* (New York: Paragon House, 1987), 143.
2. Lasker, 118.
3. Ibid., 116.
4. Gunther, 98.
5. Herbert F. Margulies, *Reconciliation and Revival: James R. Mann and the House Republicans in the Wilson Era* (Westport, Conn.: Greenwood Press, 1996), x.
6. August Hecksher, *Woodrow Wilson: A Biography* (New York: Charles Scribner's Sons, 1991), 215.
7. Arthur Link and William M. Leary Jr., "The Election of 1916," in *The Coming to Power: Critical Presidential Elections in American History* (previously published as part of *History of American Presidential Elections*), ed. Arthur M. Schlesinger Jr. (New York: Chelsea House Publishers in association with McGraw-Hill, 1971), 2257.
8. Lasker, 116.
9. "Coast Factions Unite," *New York Times,* 14 April 1918, 9.
10. Ralph M. Goldman, *The National Party Chairmen and the Committees: Factional-*

ism at the Top (Armonk, N.Y.: M. E. Sharpe, 1990), 295. Goldman's take on Roosevelt's position on the League needs clarification. He was opposed to any international organization if it required the United States, in his words, "to surrender our right and duty to prepare our own strength for our own defense." Roosevelt believed Wilson's version of the League of Nations deprived the United States of such a right.

11. Lasker, 117.
12. Gunther, 100.
13. Ibid.
14. Will H. Hays, *The Memoirs of Will H. Hays* (Garden City, N.Y.: Doubleday Press, 1955), 157.
15. Ibid.
16. "Wilson Appeals to Nation," *New York Times,* 26 October 1918, 1.
17. John Gunther Papers, Special Collections, Joseph Regenstein Library, University of Chicago, Box 99 Folder 7. The other two subheadquarters were located in Chicago and San Francisco.
18. Lasker, 120.
19. "'I Say Fight,' Is Hays' Reply to Wilson's Appeal," *New York Times,* 28 October 1918, 1.
20. Oscar Theodore Barck Jr. and Nelson Manford Blake, *Since 1900: A History of the United States in Our Times* (New York: Macmillan, 1947), 240.
21. "I Say Fight," 1.
22. Ibid.
23. "Taft and Roosevelt Appeal to Voters," *New York Times,* 1 November 1918, 4.
24. Ibid.
25. "Will Win Congress, W. H. Hays Declares," *New York Times,* 5 November 1918, 8.
26. Ibid.
27. Margulies, 287.
28. Seward W. Livermore, *Politics Is Adjourned: Woodrow Wilson and the War Congress, 1916–1918* (Middletown, Conn.: Wesleyan University Press, 1996), 224–243.
29. Margulies, 154.
30. Lasker's family had emigrated to the United States from Germany in the 1850s. Lasker himself was born in 1880, while the family was making a return visit.
31. Lasker, 124.
32. Gunther, 102. Fund-raising was to become a critical issue for Republicans between 1918–1920. Although Hays called for a limit on the amount individuals could contribute, it was occasionally ignored. According to Gunther, Lasker spent nearly $40,000 to publish and distribute *After the Peace, What?* He made other contributions and was later called to testify before a Senate committee investigating campaign financing during the 1920 presidential election.
33. "Armour Gave $5,000 to Republican Fund," *New York Times,* 30 October 1918, 11. Democrats tried to make an issue of Republican fund-raising two days earlier when the *Times* published the names of Republican contributors. The list included R. B. Mellon of Pittsburgh, who gave $2,000, and William Procter of Ohio (and Procter and Gamble), who gave $7,500. See "Charges Big Fund to Block Wilson," *New York Times,* 28 October 1918, 1. One day later the *Times* ran a story on Democratic contributors and reported the list was topped by a $25,000 donation by Bernard Baruch, chairman of the War Industries Board. See "Democratic Fund Reported $412,138," *New York Times,* 29 October 1918, 22.
34. Lasker, 128.

4
To Washington, Through Chicago

Albert Lasker returned to Chicago after the 1918 elections. However, he continued to shuttle back and forth to New York over the next two years to maintain control over the RNC's publicity department.[1] Despite the good news of the prior November, problems within the Republican Party over the League of Nations would occupy Lasker's time and energy for the foreseeable future. Shortly before his death in January 1919, Theodore Roosevelt and Henry Cabot Lodge joined forces in opposition to the League. Other Republicans threw their support to the League to Enforce Peace, headed by William Howard Taft.[2] Roosevelt's death dramatically weakened any GOP opposition to the League; it also removed him from the 1920 presidential campaign. And it created a void in Lasker's life, who not only supported Roosevelt but admired him as well: "I want to say that I am sure in my own mind, that if Colonel Roosevelt hadn't died, it was all arranged for him to have been nominated in 1920."[3] Before his death Roosevelt had tried to head off further intraparty strife, urging RNC Chairman Will Hays and GOP congressional leaders to do all they could to prevent a split. Too many good things were happening for Republicans right now that a stumble of any kind could destroy. Republicans controlled both houses of Congress and seemed perfectly positioned to recapture the White House in 1920. Equally important were the things the Republican Party was doing internally. It had truly become a national operation with year-round activities. Hays traveled constantly, speaking to groups not only at the national but state and local levels as well.

The party was also making plans to reach out to groups just beginning to grasp the extent of their political power. Once women's suffrage was granted via constitutional amendment, the RNC created a women's division at national headquarters, consisting of a general chairperson, three vice-chairpersons, and a national women's council of one hundred.[4] Appealing to women was one of Lasker's strong suits as an advertiser. He had successfully sold them on Van Camp's Pork and Beans, and would enjoy a similar triumph later on with Lucky Strike cigarettes.

Throughout the 1920 presidential campaign, and regardless of who the nominee might be, the publicity machine assembled by Will Hays and Albert Lasker was going to churn out press releases, books, pamphlets, pictures, campaign buttons, billboard and newspaper advertising, and motion picture newsreels.[5] All that the Republicans would have to do is settle on a presidential candidate.

That would prove to be easier said than done. Although the chances for victory in November 1920 seemed good, so, too, were the chances that it might seem pyrrhic as a result of a costly battle for the nomination. After Roosevelt died, the Progressive wing of the Republican Party was available to anyone who could capture it. California Senator Hiram Johnson of California, a Progressive who was strongly opposed to American involvement in the League of Nations, sought their support. He was challenged by General Leonard Wood of New Hampshire. Wood had commanded Roosevelt and his Roughriders during the Spanish-American War of 1898. By December 1919 the field of possible candidates had swollen to nine, including Ohio Senator Warren G. Harding, who was supported by Senators Boies Penrose of Pennsylvania and Reed Smoot of Utah as someone conservatives could support.[6]

Given his choice Harding would probably have preferred to continue representing Ohio in the U.S. Senate. He was elected in 1914 after a successful stint as a state senator and lieutenant governor, and his relatively undistinguished tenure on Capitol Hill was nonetheless a happy one. He carried his committee load, stayed out of trouble, and generally followed the lead of older, more conservative Republicans. Even though his legislative record was subpar, and his attendance record even worse, it seemed satisfactory to his constituents back home.[7] He was friendly, and not openly hostile to anyone. He went to great lengths to avoid conflict and claimed almost as many Democrats as Republicans in the Senate as friends. He probably would have remained in the Senate for the rest of his public life had he not felt compelled to react to events back in Ohio, events that threatened to put an end to his prestigious and seemingly carefree lifestyle.

In 1920, Harry Daugherty, an Ohio lawyer who helped Harding run the state's Republican Party, warned Harding about a rival faction within the state campaigning for Leonard Wood. The twin perils of this were that if the Wood faction, led by Cincinnati soap maker William Procter, were able to dominate the delegate selection process, it would eventually gain complete control of the party. This would mean an end to Harding's and Daugherty's control, and to Harding's Senate career. One way to protect Harding's position, reasoned Daugherty, was to have him declare for the presidency. The move might win him enough delegate support at home to hold on to the party and his Senate seat. Harding agreed, and beginning in January 1920 he made a few speeches around the state touting his candidacy. The results were not encouraging. Ohio, according to all accounts, was infatuated with the idea of Leonard Wood as president. It seemed doubtful that Harding could round up enough delegates to stem the tide. Daugherty then suggested that Harding campaign for the nomination in a few other states to be considered legitimate. That might convince Ohio voters of Harding's intentions and give a boost to his prospects back home. Again Harding agreed, entered the Indiana primary, and made a speaking tour of Texas, Missouri, Kansas, and Colorado.[8]

Harding's and Daugherty's maneuverings were taking place against the backdrop of the actions of the more seriously considered candidates. As feared, the 1920 Republican presidential primaries were nasty yet inconclusive affairs. A stalemate was building between Johnson, Wood, and Illinois Governor Frank Lowden. As for Harding, his strategy was backfiring. He did poorly in the primaries. Even though he won in Ohio, he had to share some of the delegates with Leonard Wood. To add insult to injury, Daugherty was defeated in a bid to become a delegate-at-large.[9] Harding's poor showing on the campaign trail even dried up the support from his Senate colleagues, who largely supported his candidacy from the standpoint that it would be nice to have a friend in the White House.[10]

Albert Lasker was not a Harding supporter. Harding's performance in the Senate fight against the League of Nations had made the adman suspicious: "It was essential to nominate someone opposed to the League idea to the Presidency in order to show Republicans their strength. Roosevelt had died, and many party leaders such as Taft and Charles Evans Hughes were going along with Wilson. We tried to get Senator [William] Borah to run. Borah wouldn't do it, even when Senator Johnson tried to get him to, so Johnson agreed to run."[11] Lasker, apparently unable to persuade Republicans with the written version of "reason why" advertising, would now try to bend the party to his view of the League of Nations by offering a flesh and bone version of "reason why" advertising. But he was troubled by the fact that he going to support Hiram Johnson while serving as RNC publicity chief. He felt he had to remove himself from the post in order to avoid a potentially embarrassing conflict-of-interests flap: " I went to Will Hays and said you must let me resign from the National Committee, because I'm going to back Johnson. I might embarrass you by pushing a man for the nomination while I was working for the Committee. Hays wouldn't let me resign, but did give me a leave of absence."[12]

The Hiram Johnson campaign would come to include some dynamic Progressive personalities, including Harold Ickes, Dean Acheson, Felix Frankfurter, and William Allen White.[13] The group met sporadically in the early part of 1920, sometimes at Ickes's home in Winnetka, Illinois, and at other times at Lasker's estate in nearby Glencoe.[14] Topics of the meetings included possible Progressive planks in the Republican platform, and the chances of a Progressive actually winning the nomination. Unfortunately Johnson wasn't making their job any easier. He was reluctant to campaign actively, and that reluctance cost him time and support. Some Progressives, Harold Ickes for one, got tired of waiting and went to work for Illinois Governor Frank Lowden.[15] Procter and Gamble President William Procter had become equally impatient, and declared for Leonard Wood, eventually managing his national campaign.[16] When Johnson finally got on the campaign trail, he found himself without the necessary time to build a national grassroots organization. Furthermore several primaries had already been held, and many of those delegates had gone to Wood or Lowden. To pull even with them prior to the June convention in Chicago would prove difficult and expensive, but Lasker plunged into Johnson's campaign. He oversaw publicity in the remaining primaries and contributed to the campaign. He also secured donations from other high rollers such as chewing gum executive William Wrigley Jr.[17]

In early June the Johnson campaign, accompanied by a brass band and a parade, arrived in Chicago for the Republican Convention. Lasker's candidate of choice had over one hundred delegates pledged to him, second only to Leonard Wood.[18] Still, he had no illusions about Johnson's chances. His record as a Progressive and his role as Theodore Roosevelt's running mate in 1912 hurt him in the eyes of Old Guard Republicans. He was the only presidential candidate totally opposed to the League of Nations, which pleased Lasker, but proved to be costly. Johnson's opposition to the League brought nonliberal elements into his campaign. This caused friction among liberals, who left, taking with them Johnson's claim that he was the only Progressive candidate.[19] Additionally his attacks on Lowden's and Wood's fund-raising activities, prompting a Senate investigation that uncovered lavish spending and other monetary irregularities, would probably doom his chances to snag a vice presidential nomination.[20] Still, he was hopeful that Johnson's performance in the primaries, coupled with whatever breaks he might get in a potentially stalemated convention, would convince party regulars that the anti-League faction was a force to be reckoned with, and Johnson would get the nomination.

The Republican convention opened on June 8th in the Chicago Coliseum, and it became clear very quickly that it was headed for a stalemate. Lowden, Wood, and Johnson were all jammed at the top, and with none of them showing any signs of quitting, the chances of a smooth convention followed by a smooth fall campaign appeared doubtful. It seemed like a perfect opportunity for a dark-horse candidate to make a successful play for the nomination. Remarkably, despite his dismal showing in the primaries, Warren Harding was still one of those dark-horse possibilities.[21] He had run a smart, albeit lackluster, campaign. He had not alienated any particular group within the party and had stayed out of states that featured favorite-son candidates. He was also free of the taint of fund-raising irregularities. Up to the convention Harding's campaign convention was a shoe-string operation when compared with that of Frank Lowden and Leonard Wood. Harding's heaviest hitters included Carmi Thompson, an Ohio political operative who gave him nearly $14,000, and Harvey Firestone, who gave $1,000. After that was the man who bought the newspaper Harding owned in Marion, Ohio ($800); Harding's brother George, who pitched in $500; and a neighbor, Ed Scobey, who also gave $500.[22] Harding's expenditures prior to coming to Chicago totaled just over $113,000. Frank Lowden, on the other hand, spent more than $400,000.[23] Both Harding's and Lowden's efforts were dwarfed by Leonard Wood's expenditures, which totaled $1,773,000 and earned him charges that he was trying to buy the nomination.[24] Lowden was also accused of allegedly bribing two Missouri delegates, and Wood was criticized for violating an unwritten rule not to campaign in states featuring a favorite-son candidate, as he had done against Harding in Ohio. Also in Harding's favor was his personality, which some termed boring, but which others thought might appeal to voters tired of activist presidents such as Teddy Roosevelt and Woodrow Wilson.[25] It was thought that a mediocre candidate might be the perfect antidote to the Wilson presidency. Tired of Wilson's dictatorship? Why not try an average American for a change? Someone of that description was sure to be a more suitable president than any overachiever. And

Warren Harding seemed to fit the description like a glove. He was well liked, unassuming, good natured, and the essence of conciliation and compromise. These were qualities that became more important as the convention drifted from vote to meaningless vote, and delegates, stuck in the hot, unventilated Chicago Coliseum, where temperatures climbed to over 100 degrees, searched for someone, almost anyone, to nominate and go home. Despite the rumblings about a dark-horse candidate sweeping into the convention to wrest the nomination from the front-runners, Albert Lasker and other Hiram Johnson supporters were sticking with their man: "We had taken a suite for Senator Johnson at the Blackstone Hotel. His suite was directly under the suite which is known as the 'smoke-filled room'"[26]

The "smoke-filled room" was officially listed as Suite 404 by Blackstone Hotel officials and belonged to George Harvey, publisher of *Harvey's Weekly,* and RNC Chairman Will Hays.[27] Harvey was a former Democrat turned ardent Wilson hater. Their suite became the site of principal consultations once it became clear the convention was deadlocked over Wood, Johnson, and Lowden. Talks began on the evening of Friday, June 11, four days into the convention and after the fourth ballot, in which no candidate won the necessary 493 votes to clinch the nomination. Harding's name did not initially come up in the consultations, because at this point he was actually losing delegate strength.[28] The first ballot gave him just over sixty-five votes. Four ballots later he was down by nearly four.[29]

Between 8:00 P.M. Friday and 2:00 A.M. Saturday, some sixteen present and past U.S. senators filed into and milled about Suite 404, each contributing his ideas as to how to break the logjam on the convention floor. Frank Brandegee of Connecticut was the unofficial chairman.[30] Henry Cabot Lodge was there but reportedly invested no effort on anyone's behalf.[31] Illinois Senator Medill McCormick was backing Lowden. The only senator at the time publicly pressing Harding's case was Reed Smoot of Utah.[32] Reporters who caught wind of the meeting staked out the suite and buttonholed participants as they came and went. Smoot told one he thought the convention would turn to Harding. Charles Curtis of Kansas said the same thing. Regardless of who spoke to the press, as the night wore on the message was beginning to sound the same: the frontrunners have serious liabilities that could hurt the Republican Party in November. Warren Harding seems the most available choice.[33]

One floor below, Lasker and others continued to campaign for Hiram Johnson: "If memory serves me right, Johnson felt the nomination should have been tendered to him, since our group had forced our foreign relations plank into the party platform. The night before the convention in Chicago, while the platform committee was meeting, we held a rally at which Johnson spoke. The platform committee, which was at work just across the street from the rally had felt the reverberations of this meeting. We forced that plank in."[34]

In the end the foreign policy plank's final wording, written by moderate Elihu Root and adopted by the convention, offered something for everyone; it endorsed the principle of the League of Nations but referred to it instead as an international association. It likewise denounced the League as proposed by President Wilson as un-American and dangerous to American sovereignty. It justified the opposition of Republican senators to this League, whether that opposition was voiced against the whole treaty or in the form of reservations intended to safeguard American interests. This blanket clause, denouncing the Wilson treaty and the League plan, was so worded as to take within its language every Republican in the Senate, irreconcilable or reservationist.[35] The League plank would prove to be a blessing to Harding, who, despite his support of Lodge in the Senate battles against the League, was not a fervent isolationist.[36] It would, however, be a curse to other Republicans, who would spend the fall campaign either trying to figure out just where Harding stood on the issue or trying to make sure his views remained purposely obscure. It would be especially troubling for Lasker. To him, the wording of the foreign policy plank was the equivalent of a virtual sellout of his position. He concluded that whoever the GOP nominated, Johnson excluded, would not oppose the League of Nations as strongly as he would like. In the end even Hiram Johnson let him down. Anxious to make himself acceptable to Old Guard Republicans in control of the convention, he toned down his League position and showed a willingness to go along with the party platform.[37] Lasker felt disillusioned, and began to think about quitting his RNC position once the convention was over.

But that would have to wait until the business in Suite 404 was completed. On Saturday, June 12, at 2:45 A.M., Warren Harding was told that he was about to become the compromise candidate of the Republican Party.[38] One floor below, Lasker and other Hiram Johnson supporters, waiting in Johnson's suite, were about to get the news from an unlikely messenger: "About three or four of us were in his suite about two o'clock in the morning the day the nomination was made when Senator Harding came in. That was the first time I met Harding. He [Harding] said he wanted to talk to Johnson alone, and they went into the bedroom. They talked for five or ten minutes, and when Harding left, Johnson was livid with anger. He said, 'I like Harding. I like him very much, but I can't conceive of him being President of the United States. He's done nothing to deserve it. He tells me they have just agreed upstairs to make him President, and he came down here to ask me, wouldn't I run as Vice President?'"[39] Lasker was also troubled by Harding's selection, not only because of the way the selection was handled but also because Lasker knew they disagreed on the League issue. It threatened to add an element of suspicion and mistrust in their working relationship once the fall campaign started.

The convention reconvened later that morning. Delegates, unable to find overnight relief from the heat (a condition aggravated by too little air conditioning and too much Prohibition), tramped back into the auditorium to resume voting. They took their seats on wooden chairs that oozed sticky, raw pine pitch as a result of the hot, humid conditions inside the Chicago Coliseum.[40] Rumors that the deadlock was going to be broken fanned their interest. Ballots five through seven revealed no apparent change, as Frank Lowden and Leonard Wood continued to lead the pack of possible nominees. However, neither had enough support to be considered the clear front-runner. Hiram Johnson was running third in the balloting, and Warren Harding was fifth with 78 delegates. On the sixth ballot, Harding picked up another 11 votes and now had 89, but he was still too far back to be considered a possibility. The seventh ballot was a different story. This time Harding's delegate count was 105, placing him fourth behind Wood, Lowden, and Johnson. By the eighth ballot, Harding had picked up 133 delegates, and panic spread simultaneously through the Wood and Lowden camps. Both parties pestered Convention Chairman Henry Cabot Lodge and RNC Chairman Will Hays until a forty-five-minute recess was called at 4:00 P.M. The Lowden and Wood forces used the time to evaluate the situation. A trend didn't seem to be forming for Harding, but something was happening. He had picked up a trickle of support from the Missouri, Indiana, New York, Wyoming, Alabama, and Texas delegations.[41] Fearing that a trickle could turn into a torrent, the Lowden and Wood forces met to head off the chance of some serious political hemorrhaging happening on the convention floor. Their inability to break their own impasse proved disastrous to both sides when the balloting resumed shortly before 5:00 P.M. The ninth ballot saw Harding break through the Wood-Lowden logjam, in the process destroying not only Lowden's dream of snagging the nomination, but also Hiram Johnson's. Johnson had begun the day with 116 delegates. By the ninth ballot he had fallen to 82, been lumped into the also-ran category, and was just one ballot round away from convention oblivion. But the real casualty of the ninth ballot seemed to be Frank Lowden. He led all contenders at the end of the eighth round with 307 delegates. The political landscape beneath his feet began shifting at the start of the ninth ballot, and the shift cost him 60 percent of his delegate strength. The move to Harding seemed to be happening at his expense. The Connecticut delegation moved first, as Frank Brandegee led all but one of his state's delegates to Harding. The Florida delegation followed suit. By the time the roll call got to Kentucky, Lowden's campaign was disintegrating. Alvin Hert, head of the Kentucky delegation, and Lowden's campaign manager, released his delegates. Moments later all 26 of Kentucky's delegates pledged their allegiance to Harding. They were followed by all of Louisiana's delegates, the portion of the Missouri contingent that hadn't gone to Harding earlier, and 66 of New York's 88 votes. Clearly the move was on. Harding now had over 374 votes, and his supporters were warning other delegations to get on the train or risk being left behind at the station. Holdout states began to fall in line on the tenth ballot, and when the Pennsylvania delegation threw most of its votes to Harding, it was all over. The final tally gave Harding a fraction over 692 votes, followed by Leonard Wood at 156, Hiram Johnson with a shade under 81, and Frank Lowden with 11.[42] Few delegates heard the official results, many having dashed to the exits and cooler air.[43]

It was Harry Daugherty's dream that Harding's nomination would be helped by Republican power brokers once they realized they had a deadlocked convention on their hands. It was a dream he shared with reporters, and the dream found its way into the *New York Times* February 21, 1920, edition. The dream nearly became a nightmare for the GOP four months later, when it had to defend itself against charges a "Senate cabal" had orchestrated Harding's selection. Clearly, the activities in Suite 404 and its adjacent hallway didn't put to rest fears that something unethical had taken place. Lasker felt something illicit had occurred, prompting him to consider quitting the Republican National Committee. But the real question at the bottom of the controversy is whether Harding could have been nominated without alleged tampering by GOP leaders in that so-called smoke-filled room.

There may not have been a "smoke-filled" hotel room in Harding's journey to the presidency, but there was a hotel room. In fact there were two of them. The one at the Blackstone Hotel in Chicago has gotten its share of attention, but a room in the Wardman Park Hotel in Washington, D.C., also had a bearing on Harding's future. It belonged to Boies Penrose, the senior senator from Pennsylvania, who in the summer of 1919 took it upon himself to find a presidential candidate. He was looking for someone with whom conservative Republican senators could work, and most likely do their bidding. He was also worried about Leonard Wood. Republican Progressives were gravitating toward Wood in the wake of Theodore Roosevelt's death. They seemed energized, and that spelled trouble for Old Guard Republicans such as Penrose. Penrose eventually settled on Harding as someone who could stand up to Wood, as well as go along with the party elders. He invited Harding up to his room one day, had him take off his coat, make himself comfortable, and then asked him if he would like to be president of the United States. Harding, stunned by the offer, tried to beg off. He had cash flow and political problems at home that needed attention. But Penrose would have none of that: "I'll look after all that. You will make the McKinley type of candidate. You look the part. You can make a front porch campaign like McKinley and we'll do the rest."[44]

Penrose's offer and his assessment of Harding's chances were not that far off. To him, Harding looked like presidential material and would be a safe bet for the Republican Party in 1920. Harding wasn't a boat rocker; Penrose felt confident Harding would listen to him and other leaders and do what he was asked. That may be one key in trying to unlock the mystery of how Warren Harding, possessing some latent presidential ambitions but riddled with doubts about his chances, managed to become the Republican nominee for president. He wasn't a troublemaker. When he arrived in the Senate, he took the advice of senior members and was seen but rarely heard. On the few occasions he parted company with party leaders on legislative issues, it was not so much a result of ideological differences, but because he had an uncanny sense of what would play with Ohio voters. He supported the women's suffrage and prohibition movements not because he believed in them, but rather because he thought voters ought to have the final word. His support of the amendments would speed them on to the public arena, where his constituents could decide their fate. Regardless of what happened, he would at least have given voters their chance to be heard on the issues. In the process he was also neatly dodging two explosive political issues that could come back to haunt him down the road. In general he was the type of person who went out of his way to be agreeable and friendly to all he met. Few senators had a bad word to say about him. His behavior seemed to suggest he was modest, unassuming, and good-natured, as well as friendly. Harding had traveled the presidential preconvention trail carefully, displaying just the right amount of reluctance and humility to offset whatever presidential ambitions he truly harbored.[45] As the nominee Harding could do what neither Lowden, Wood, or Johnson could, that is, parlay his apparent ambivalence on issues such as the League of Nations into something that would hold together all wings of the Republican Party until

November. He truly seemed to be the essence of conciliation and compromise.

Looking back it might be fair to say the Washington hotel encounter may have nurtured Harding's presidential chances. But what about the smoke-filled hotel room in Chicago? Did senators proclaim a nominee or merely the obvious? A brief analysis of who really picked Harding would seem to indicate that convention delegates knew more than their leaders.

Even though Warren Harding may not have been a household name to voters in 1920, most of the delegates in Chicago knew who he was. Of the 984 delegates on hand, 10 percent were veterans of the 1912 convention and heard Harding nominate William Howard Taft. Over one-fifth of the Chicago delegates had also been delegates in 1916. There they elected Harding chairman of the convention and heard him deliver the keynote address, in which he pleaded for reconciliation and party unity.[46] But three additional facts could also throw the brokered convention theory into question. First, of the 984 delegates assembled in Chicago in 1920, nearly half of them were uncommitted, meaning they could vote for any candidate they chose.[47] Second, the need to have Ohio in the Republican column in November was of critical importance. The National Association of Republican State Chairmen, meeting in Washington in December 1919, agreed that a candidate was needed to guarantee that state in 1920. That alone gave Harding an obvious edge.[48] Finally, the senators and other power brokers who met in Chicago the night of June 11 may have concluded that the real problem was not a convention out of control, but a convention beyond theirs. The delegates liked Harding and seemed inclined to nominate him if given the chance. To block that move would expose the senators to real charges of trying to rig the nomination. To get in front of the delegates to lead them in a direction in which they were already headed would at least project to the nation an image of the senators being back in the driver's seat. And speaking of national image, Harding had one that could seemingly be made up and not covered up as the campaign went along. Other candidates would need more work in order to make them attractive to voters. Wood, Lowden, and Johnson had all hurt themselves in the eyes of potential voters. They had tried at various times during the convention to secure the nomination by brokering deals among themselves. Lowden and Wood were already fending off charges they had tried to buy the nomination. Had Johnson been nominated, he would have found it difficult to win the support of Old Guard Republicans, who remembered his defection to Teddy Roosevelt and the Progressive Party in 1912. Given all that, Warren Harding was not just the available man, as some have called him, but the inevitable candidate of the Republican Party. If there were any remaining suspicions about the efforts of a "Senate cabal" to orchestrate the convention, thirteen of the sixteen senators present in that Chicago hotel room went out the next day and proceeded to vote against Warren Harding until the ninth ballot. By that time the delegate shift to Harding was underway.[49]

Even though most of the Republican Party may have embraced Warren Harding, Lasker didn't. The day after Harding had been nominated, Lasker huddled with and sought the advice of a few other dejected Republicans. Among them were Ruth McCormick, whose husband Medill had backed Frank Lowden, and Alice Roosevelt, who had never forgiven Harding for a public attack he had unleashed on her father at the 1912 convention. Lasker's problem with Harding, beyond the question of his mysterious rise to power, was his position on the League of Nations. So far as Lasker could tell, Harding had merely given lip service to his opposition, but at heart was really for it.[50] He decided he'd had enough, and planned to leave politics altogether and return to Lord & Thomas. Before he could resign his RNC position, he received a call from Will Hays, who had gone to Harding's hometown of Marion at the candidate's request. Harding asked him to remain as head of the RNC. He then wanted to know if there was anyone else at the RNC he should immediately meet. Hays suggested a meeting with Lasker, because he was in charge of the publicity department. Harding agreed and summoned the advertising executive: "He asked me to remain on the job, in the same capacity I had occupied before the convention. I said, 'I'm glad to remain, because there is a major issue involved, in which I am deeply interested—that is the defeat of the League of Nations. I can assure you that you can absolutely trust me, so long as you're against the League. I want to tell you, in fairness to both of us, don't trust me at all, if I ever feel you are no longer wholly against it. I might use my position to embarrass you.'"[51] It was not idle chatter and was not meant to be. Lasker had spent nearly $40,000 of his own money to help the GOP publish pamphlets warning of the dangers of League involvement. He had, with another sizeable donation of money and time, supported Hiram Johnson's efforts to gain control of the party on this issue. He had also enlisted the help of other prominent people such as William Wrigley Jr. and publisher William Randolph Hearst.[52] Lasker was not to be taken lightly. Apparently unable to accurately gauge Lasker's intense feelings on the subject, Harding responded ambiguously to the warning by saying he thought friendship should transcend politics. "Lasker," he said, "let's agree at the start on one thing; that we'll never fall out because we disagree."[53] It was a subtle warning to Lasker that Harding would have to be watched on the League issue. It would seem that "wiggle and wobble," a phrase Lasker often used to characterize indecision by others, and which would become a campaign slogan with which to attack Democrats, could just as accurately be applied to his own candidate. Lasker was determined not to let Harding wiggle or wobble on the League issue.

NOTES

1. Lasker, 122.
2. Goldman, 291.
3. Lasker, 122.
4. Goldman, 291.
5. Ibid., 294.
6. Ibid., 297. Harding's support in the Senate was also fueled by Leonard Wood's campaign activities. Wood had challenged favorite sons Frank Lowden and Warren Harding in their own states, which at the time was a political sin of the highest order. For more on the Senate's efforts to stop Wood, see Wesley M. Bagby, *The Road to Normalcy: The Presidential Campaign and Election of 1920* (Baltimore: Johns Hopkins University Press, 1967), 28.
7. Murray, 15.
8. Ibid., 29.

9. Mark Sullivan, *Our Times: America at the Birth of the Twentieth Century* (New York: Charles Scribner's Sons, 1933), 593.

10. Ibid. Sullivan also reports that Harding's presidential chances looked so bleak that at the convention in Chicago he hedged his bets and refiled for the U.S. Senate race in Ohio. He beat the deadline by less than two minutes.

11. Lasker, 125.

12. Ibid.

13. Arthur M. Schlesinger, *The Crisis of the Old Order, 1919–1933* (Boston: Houghton Mifflin, 1956), 26. White later left the Johnson campaign, complaining it had been highjacked by conservatives and was no longer progressive.

14. Lasker had a number of residences in the Chicago area. For years he lived near the University of Chicago before moving to the part of the city called the Gold Coast. The Glencoe estate was used primarily as a summer residence until 1926 when he moved permanently to a 400-acre site in Lake Forest.

15. Harold Ickes, *The Autobiography of a Curmudgeon* (New York: Reynal & Hitchcock, 1943), 228.

16. Ibid.

17. Ickes, 230.

18. Murray, 31. The delegate support was all the more impressive given the fact that Johnson's late start caused him to miss ten of twenty-two primaries.

19. Bagby, 32.

20. Actually Lasker was mistaken about Johnson's viability as a vice presidential nominee. On the night of June 11th, Lowden, Wood, and Harding all asked Johnson to be their vice president. He said no to all of them.

21. In reality Harding was less of a dark horse than people thought. Shortly after Teddy Roosevelt's death, the *New York Tribune* pronounced Harding the only Old Guard Republican that Progressives could support. The *New York Post* reported his candidacy was the talk of most politicians in Washington, and RNC Chairman Will Hays was quoted that because of his strong base in the Middle West and his popularity on Wall Street, Harding was the most likely choice. For more on Harding's chances, see Bagby, 40.

22. Murray, 28.

23. Of that $400,000, Lowden spent $16,000 to establish a women's division in his campaign. For more on Lowden's campaign expenditures, see William T. Hutchinson, *Lowden of Illinois: The Life of Governor Frank O. Lowden,* vol. 1 (Chicago: University of Chicago Press, 1957), 57–60.

24. Murray, 30–31. Much of Lowden's funding came from his wife's family, who were heirs to the Pullman fortune. For more on preconvention spending by the Republicans, see Eugene P. Trani, *The Presidency of Warren G. Harding* (Lawrence: Regents Press of Kansas, 1977), 21–22.

25. Goldman, 298.

26. Lasker, 128.

27. Murray, 37. Harvey later became ambassador to Great Britain.

28. Hays, 248.

29. Richard C. Bain, *Convention Decisions and Voting Records* (Washington, D.C., Brookings Institution, 1960), Appendix D.

30. Hays, 249.

31. Ibid. In his memoirs, Hays seemed to recall Lodge supporting Leonard Wood.

32. Murray, 38.

33. Ibid.

34. Lasker, 129.

35. Hays, 247.

36. Murray, 15.
37. Bagby, 33.
38. Hays, 247. A delegation led by George Harvey met with Harding to ask if there was anything in his personal life that might hurt his chances to become president. Harding thought about it for a few moments and said no. It's possible the senators were interested in knowing if Harding had committed the kind of fund-raising errors that had derailed the Lowden and Wood campaigns. It's also possible that Harding never thought about his extramarital affairs or considered them campaign liabilities. They would come to occupy the time of a good many RNC officials, including Albert Lasker.
39. Lasker, 131.
40. Murray, 3.
41. Ibid.
42. Bain, Appendix D.
43. Murray, 5.
44. Francis Russell, *The Shadow of Blooming Grove: Warren G. Harding in His Times* (New York: McGraw-Hill, 1968), 330. Some of the political problems bothering Harding was the growing power of the Wood campaign in Ohio, which threatened to seize control of the Ohio Republican Party and jeopardize his Senate seat.
45. Murray, 40.
46. Bain, 326.
47. Harold F. Alderfer, "The Personality and Politics of Warren G. Harding" (Ph.D. diss., Syracuse University, 1928), 34.
48. Russell, 335.
49. Murray, 35.
50. Lasker, 131.
51. Ibid., 133.
52. W. A. Swanberg, *Citizen Hearst: A Biography of William Randolph Hearst* (New York: Charles Scribner's Sons, 1961), 333. Like Lasker, Hearst was also skeptical of Johnson's chances and urged him to launch a third-party campaign.
53. Lasker, 133.

5
Something Old, Something New . . .

Warren Harding's election as president in 1920 would end eight years of Democratic Party control of the White House. It would also signal that a new alliance had been forged between politics and modern advertising. Albert Lasker would prove to be one of the bridges connecting the two institutions. What's interesting about Lasker's efforts are the efforts of others to trivialize them. John Gunther, Lasker's biographer, gives little insight as to just what Lasker did for Harding and the Republicans that year. Lasker's own reminiscences, dictated to Columbia University in 1950, contain little that would be considered helpful. That was in keeping with Lasker's approach to his advertising work—promote the product, not the promoter. The only significant caches of material regarding Lasker's political exploits are Warren Harding's papers, held by the Ohio Historical Society, and the Will Hays Papers, held by the Indiana State Library. Secondary sources include Robert Murray's *The Harding Era: Warren G. Harding and His Administration* (1969) and Randolph Downes's *The Rise of Warren Gamaliel Harding, 1865-1920* (1970). Despite the efforts of many to diminish Lasker's role in 1920, evidence persists that he was a significant player who deserves more coverage than he has received so far. He became a power unto himself during the campaign, responsible and accountable only to RNC Chairman Will Hays. He rarely floated any ideas through channels; he either went directly to Hays or sometimes bypassed him and went to Harding himself. And there were times when he simply relied on his advertising instincts and did what he thought was best. This occasionally meant acting without the knowledge or approval of either Hays or Harding and left the impression with many inside and out of the Republican Party that Lasker was making the campaign conform to his vision, and not the other way around. Lasker did all this even though he had very little professional respect for the man he was helping to elect. He distrusted Warren Harding on the League of Nations issue. He also found Harding's sexual indiscretions, some of which he would be asked to help minimize, to be troubling. Still, a client was a client. Even a president who wasn't completely against the League was better than a president who was completely for it.

Although most of the overall planning of the Harding campaign would be handled by Will Hays, Harry Daugherty, and, to a surprising degree, Warren Harding, Lasker's influence would be felt with regard to the plan's execution as well as the packaging and presenting of the candidate. He packaged Harding in such a way as to help humanize him, magnifying those assets the strategists thought most appealing and reducing flaws and possible campaign gaffes to their barest minimum. Packaging and presentation would also feature new advertising and technological achievements: Lasker's use of "reason why" advertising, market research and segmentation, and the use of the movie camera and the phonograph, to mention a few. But before all these new ideas could step forward and claim center stage in American political life, they would first have to be ushered onstage by older, more traditional techniques so as not to jar the voter. It was this blending of old and new, presided over by Lasker, that resulted in Warren Harding's election.

The "old" was the use of the front-porch campaign. It was a more dignified way of soliciting votes, and was in keeping with the image GOP strategists wanted to portray of Harding's "seemliness."[1] Harding himself agreed with the strategy: "It develops an unfortunate side of our political activities to have a presidential candidate chasing about the country soliciting support. One cannot be his best in conveying his thoughts to the people whose confidence he desires to enlist. Let the undignified [James] Cox do this, and, by so doing, place himself on the defensive in the eyes of people of good taste."[2] It also meshed with two Republican objectives. The first was to showcase Harding as a folksy, hardworking small town American who preferred Main Street to Pennsylvania Avenue.[3] Republicans had accurately gauged the public's weariness of the passions of war, intraparty strife, and the highbrow intellectualism personified by Woodrow Wilson.[4] The country was ready for a regular fellow, not another stuffed shirt.[5] Someone who enjoyed puttering around his office or playing cards with friends would speak volumes about the humble, sincere, and average qualities of a man seeking to become president of the United States. What better place to showcase all that than on the front porch of his own house, surrounded by neighbors who could attest to those qualities and who would welcome the devout traveling to see for themselves? It had worked for William McKinley in 1896, Benjamin Harrison in 1888, and James Garfield in 1880, so Republican leaders, including Harding, were confident it could work again in 1920. The parallels were inescapable. After all, Garfield, McKinley, and Harding were all from Ohio. The connection would be impossible for voters to miss. But the GOP wasn't taking any chances. Harding's home got a McKinley-like makeover. The front porch was extended to match McKinley's in order to accommodate visiting delegations, and the very flagpole found in McKinley's front yard was uprooted and moved to the front of Harding's Marion residence.[6]

The second GOP objective was to keep Harding from verbally shooting himself in the foot on the campaign trail. Republican leaders were worried about Harding's mental abilities.[7] He had been labeled by Connecticut Senator Frank Brandegee as "the best of the second raters," an oblique reference to Harding's intelligence as well as to the fact that he had emerged from a crowded field of candidates devoid of high-profile political luminaries such as Teddy Roosevelt. Although having a candidate whose activities would lower the body politics' pulse rate was one of the reasons why Harding appealed to the GOP, power brokers were unsure he could hold his own out on the stump. Pennsylvania Senator Boies Penrose was brutally blunt on the subject: "Keep Warren at home," he said. "Don't let him make any speeches. If he goes out on tour, somebody's sure to ask him some questions, and Warren's just the sort of damn fool that'll try to answer them."[8] So it seemed that Lasker wasn't the only person suspicious about Harding's stand on various issues. A front-porch campaign "assured a correct public version of deliberate statements."[9] It meant that the GOP could control what Harding said and what was said to him.

In order to manipulate what on the surface seemed to be an innocent, old-fashioned front-porch campaign, a very modern campaign management structure was planned out and fitted into place. The scheme included an elaborate chain of command. Republican National Committee Chairman Will Hays stationed himself in New York not only to monitor overall progress but also to keep a close eye on developments in the East. Of particular concern were New York and Pennsylvania, which between them had over 4.5 million popular and eighty-three electoral votes. Fred Upham, RNC treasurer, was based in Chicago, along with Harry New, in charge of the National Speaker's Bureau. Hays also staffed RNC outposts in Kansas City and San Francisco.[10] Albert Lasker continued to shuttle between Chicago and New York, with frequent stops in Marion. Scott Bone and Judson Welliver were listed as being directly responsible for handling publicity in Marion, but did so under Lasker's direction. Bone had built a career as a journalist of some significance with newspapers on the West Coast. Welliver's credits included stints with the *New York Sun,* where he served not only as its London correspondent during World War I, but also as its manager of European operations.[11]

How the GOP handled the media during the campaign is an important issue because it paralleled the way it handled the candidate. If party leaders were worried what might come out of Warren Harding's mouth, they were just as worried about how the press would handle it. A front-porch campaign promised not only control over the candidate but also a degree of control over the press. They would be cooped up in Marion and hungry for news and feature items to keep their readers and their editors happy. Lasker, Bone, and Welliver understood what the press needed and communicated those needs to GOP leaders. Consequently, the front-porch campaign events in Marion blended just the right amount of news and feature material to keep everyone happy. Event planners insisted that speakers representing the various visiting delegations submit their remarks days in advance for preapproval and any last minute modifications.[12] Organizers wanted to ensure the message was in keeping with what the campaign wanted disseminated by the press, but also to make sure it was done in a newsworthy fashion. It was also done to make sure there were no surprise statements that would require Harding to respond off the cuff and blunder in the process. The Harding campaign went to great lengths to mollify the press and to ensure the reasons why Harding should be elected got into print for all to read. It built a three-room press office behind George Christian's house, Harding's next door neighbor, who later became his personal secretary.

Harding, the old newspaperman he was, knew himself what the reporters needed. Once, and sometimes twice, a day he strolled into the press bungalow and held impromptu news conferences. Most of it was for the record and could be published. Those topics deemed off the record rarely if ever found their way into print.[13] No one wanted to lose access to the kind of information only Warren Harding could provide. Even Lasker helped out, responding to the press's request that the Harding campaign supply it with an automobile. "I told them they were perfectly right," Lasker said in a letter to Will Hays. "Whatever they wanted in the way of facilities, they should have, and our most important business was to keep them happy. So I am buying a new Marmon today and sending it up there; it will not cost the Committee any money."[14]

The good press relations cultivated by the Harding campaign paid dual dividends. First, by literally spoonfeeding the media what it wanted the public to know, the campaign in effect co-opted the press into an unofficial publicity arm of the Republican Party. It made Harding accessible to the press and used the intimacy of those meetings to put Harding's warmth and personality on exhibit and to communicate the reasons why Harding should be the next president of the United States. In many respects, Lasker and the Republican Party made Harding as much a spokesman for the campaign as he was the candidate. The fact the GOP brought the news to the press rather than make the press search for it contributed to another dividend. When reporters in Marion did get wind of bad news, such as Harding's extramarital affairs or allegations about his racial background, they were less inclined to write about it without first checking with campaign officials. Often the campaign would either dismiss it as Democrat propaganda, or when it became apparent there was a degree of substance to a story, reporters in Marion simply passed the news on to their editors and let them decide whether to print it.

The Harding campaign had a measure of control over news dissemination their Democratic Party rivals did not enjoy, and it was reluctant to surrender that advantage unless it became absolutely necessary. Being out on the campaign stump was risky business. Harding's handlers couldn't predict what questions he'd encounter while he was out there or construct an effective on-the-spot damage control scenario.

So, from the end of July until the middle of October 1920, Marion, Ohio, became a Mecca of sorts for the Republican faithful and the equally faithful press. Pilgrims to the shrine on Mt. Vernon Avenue, soon to be renamed Victory Way, included farmers, lumberjacks, schoolteachers, newspaper editors, politicians, religious groups, and even delegations representing entire states.[15] It would be Lasker's job to make sure those front-porch events were milked for everything they were worth in terms of publicity and their value for getting the GOP's message across. He was responsible for, among other things, supplying the bands that welcomed the visiting delegations upon their arrival in Marion, the movie and still picture coverage that documented the proceedings, and the balloons, streamers, and pictures of Harding, his wife, and father that helped to color every

Something Old, Something New . . .   53

event.[16] It would also be Lasker's job to make sure Harding didn't stray too far from Republican rhetoric during the campaign, at least in word if not in deed. He remained suspicious about Harding's League position, and that suspicion seemed to be spreading among GOP leaders. When party leaders arrived in Marion on July 22 to participate in ceremonies officially notifying Harding he'd been nominated, a subtle war of words broke out between the candidate and some of his supporters. Henry Cabot Lodge fired the first warning shot about the League across the candidate's front porch. Senate Republicans on the whole had been opposed to the League as envisioned by Woodrow Wilson. In his official remarks, Lodge reminded the candidate that "[s]uch has been the policy of the Republican Party as represented in the Senate, and such its policy will remain. We are certain that you who helped so largely to frame this policy will, when the executive authority comes into your hands, carry it out."[17] In his remarks Harding said, "Republicans favored international cooperation in peacefully solving world problems, but not through the League. A League, yes. But not this one."[18]

The message, or more accurately, the warning to Harding was clear: do not oppose the Senate and campaign against the League. But Lasker wasn't satisfied with letting Harding off with just a warning. He had issued one of his own about League when he first met the candidate, only to see it trivialized into near nothingness. Lasker took it upon himself to be constantly looking over Harding's shoulder on the League issue: "Once or twice during the campaign there came to my desk a release of a speech that Mr. Harding was going to make in which he straddled the League issue. Mr. Harding's speech writers were [Utah Senator] George Sutherland, a subsequent Supreme Court Justice, and Richard Washburn Child, subsequently Ambassador to Italy. As the three of us were like-minded, we changed the manuscript before releasing it, so as to minimize the straddle to nothingness. If we hadn't been on the job, he [Harding] would have gone much, much further toward the League."[19]

Beyond the League issue, there was little else Albert Lasker concerned himself with except getting Warren Harding the kind of publicity he needed to win election. The front-porch campaigns seemed a perfect vehicle for Harding where he could stay on the steps and portray himself, as RNC Chairman Will Hays said, as "a reassuring voice in a perplexed hour."[20] Harding's wife Florence, who proved to be an important if unheralded player in the publicity war, liked the front porch idea (and may have even suggested it in the first place) as a way to let people know that "we [she and her husband] were 'just folks.'"[21] Untold numbers of organizations put in requests to visit Marion and see Harding speak from his front porch. Every day was crowded with a visit from at least one or more delegations, who were met with a band at the train station and paraded up to Harding's house. They crowded into the front yard, trampling the grass and flowers. When it rained, the yard was a sea of mud, so campaign officials replaced what was left of the lawn with gravel. Once the crowd was settled in, the photo opportunity began. Still photography, as well as film, were important tools in this campaign. The GOP spent $200,000 alone on still photos of Harding with his wife and father, greeting delegation leaders, or raising or lowering the flag in the front yard.[22] Even if the scheduled delegation didn't show up, the show still went on. Because the group's remarks had been delivered ahead of time, a staffer simply read them aloud to Harding and gave him a chance to respond in front of the media. He then posed for the photographers, who recorded the image on film and sent it to newspapers across the country.

So it went from late July until mid October. Two front-porch events in particular stand out as bearing Lasker's personal touch. Lasker, who championed "reason why" advertising as a new way to promote politics and politicians, would now introduce two other commercial techniques: the testimonial and the preemptive ad. The first event involved the use of show-business personalities to endorse Harding. Americans had become accustomed to seeing vaudeville and movie stars drum up support for Liberty Bond sales during World War I, but few celebrities had cast themselves in the role of partisan spokespersons for a candidate. Commercially, Lasker was one of the first advertising executives to recognize the power of film and later radio as a way to advertise products. His radio pioneering would lead to some high moments in entertainment history. The *Amos 'n' Andy Show* was created by Lord & Thomas as a medium to advertise Pepsodent Toothpaste. Later a young comedian named Bob Hope was given a chance to make a success of another radio show sponsored by Pepsodent and orchestrated by Lord & Thomas. Bing Crosby and Frank Sinatra reached their first national audiences through Lord & Thomas's sponsored radio shows. The agency also introduced the first broadcasts by the Metropolitan Opera and the first chain sponsorship of football games.[23] Even though the technology for radio broadcasting had not reached a point in 1920 that would make it a valuable campaign tool, the parallel technology of voice and film had, and it would be used by Lasker to help advertise Harding.[24] In fact many of the actors and actresses who joined the Harding-Coolidge Theatrical League were making the transition from vaudeville to the vinyl disc or the silver screen. They included Mary Pickford, Douglas Fairbanks, Lillian Russell, Lillian Gish, Ethyl Barrymore, Pearl White, and Pauline Frederick.[25] Al Jolson served as the League's president.[26] The group campaigned nationally on Harding's behalf and participated in one of the more memorable front-porch events. On August 24, trains carrying seventy League members arrived in Marion from Chicago and New York. They marched from the train station to Harding's home on Mount Vernon Avenue, now renamed Victory Way, escorted by a local band, Harding supporters, visitors, Marionites, and starstruck movie fans. When they reached Harding's home they posed for pictures on the porch with the candidate, including one of Al Jolson having a flower pinned to his lapel by Florence Harding.[27] Finally, to crown the day's events, members of the Harding-Coolidge Theatrical League serenaded the Hardings with a song written by Jolson, a little number entitled "Harding, You're The Man For Us":[28]

> We need a man to guide us
> Who'll always stand beside us,
> One who is a fighter through and through
> A man who'll make the White House
> Shine out just like a lighthouse
> And Mister Harding, we've selected you.

Something Old, Something New . . .

> Harding, lead the G.O.P.
> Harding, on to Victory!
> We're here to make a fuss!
> Mister Harding, you're the man for us!
>
> We know we'll always find him
> With Coolidge right behind him
> And Coolidge never fails, you must agree
> We know he will be guarding
> The Nation just like Harding
> When they are both in Washington, D.C.
>
> Harding, Coolidge is your mate
> Harding, lead the ship of state,
> You'll get the people's vote
> And you'll also get the Donkey's goat![29]

Afterward Jolson and a few other celebrities had lunch inside the house, followed by a singalong, poster autographing, and park reception.[30] Harding himself used the event to get in a little campaigning of his own, using show business as a metaphor: "I would like the American stage to be like American citizenship, the best in the world. We have been drifting lately under one-lead activities, and I am sure the American people are going to welcome a change in the bill. For the supreme offering we need an all-star cast, presenting America to all the world."[31] The endorsement of Harding was intended to give rank-and-file voters first person "reasons why" Harding was the preferred candidate of the entertainment community.

The second front-porch event didn't really take place on Harding's porch but still had a lot to do with Harding's image. Lasker and Will Hays had decided to make extensive use of not only still photography but also motion pictures throughout the campaign. In fact, when the RNC was putting together a publicity budget, the estimated $1,346,500 it was going to spend on newspaper ads, pamphlets, lithographs, campaign buttons, and billboards also included a stipend for movie filming.[32] Footage would be taken of Harding as he went about his day, not just campaigning for president, but being Warren Harding. Both Lasker and Hays realized that in the final analysis, what was going to make their publicity effective and the campaign ultimately successful was Warren Harding himself. If the publicity was deemed credible, it was because the object of the publicity was himself credible. The publicity didn't have to create an image, because it was already there; it was touchable and accessible. Warren Harding never pretended to be more than what he always was.[33] What the publicity needed to do was make sure Harding and his qualities were known to all. If Lasker made any mistake at all in advertising Harding to voters across the country, it was perhaps to make a virtue out of reality. Lasker may have just overdone it, giving the voting public a reason to expect too much from someone who was all too human—as even Lasker would soon discover.

In any event a camera crew was stationed on a semipermanent basis in Marion and captured Warren Harding in all types of activities. There was plenty of footage of him welcoming visiting delegations as they arrived on his front porch. The camera also caught him as he discharged his duties as editor of the *Marion Star* and joked with his employees. His father was still a practicing doctor, and occasionally Harding drove him by horse-drawn carriage as he made his house calls. The event seemed a perfect film opportunity, and was duly recorded. There were also clips of him voting on Ohio primary day and supervising the distribution of post–World War I government surplus supplies.[34] The clips would then be developed, duplicated, and shipped to movie houses nationwide. For a candidate who for the time being wasn't campaigning any further than his front porch, Warren Harding was getting around, thanks to the motion picture camera. And people seemed to like what they were seeing: "Senator Harding is almost a two to one choice among the moving picture patrons of Syracuse," according to Irene Corbally, screen editor of the *Syracuse Herald,* which conducted a straw vote taken at two of the city's leading picture houses. The return from one theater gave Harding 1,664 votes to 824 for James Cox, his Democratic opponent. The second theater reported Harding received 2,258 votes to 1,219 for Cox.[35]

Lasker soon discovered that in some movie houses across the country the image people were getting of Harding was not what he or the RNC wanted them to see. They saw Harding, of course. But in addition to seeing him vote, work, or campaign, moviegoers were also seeing him play golf, considered at the time to be an elitist sport. It worried Lasker that the image might give voters the wrong idea about this folksy, friendly man from Marion, and even get them to change their minds about voting for him. If that idea was worrying Lasker, it was also beginning to gnaw at other Republican leaders. Hays got wind of the problem in a letter from Iowa Senator William Kenyon. Kenyon told of a night spent at the movies where one of the golf clips was shown, which produced "not a handclap save once. I don't believe the golf business arouses any enthusiasm."[36] The bad news traveled fast, and within a week Lasker was sharing his worries with his friend Walter Friedlander, owner of the Cincinnati Reds baseball club: "It [the golf clip] has drawn a perfectly surprising amount of unfavorable reaction around the country. We get hundreds of letters saying it's a rich man's sport."[37]

Lasker began thinking about how he could quickly put Harding in the best possible light with the greatest number of voters, and in the process eliminate the golf blunder. His solution was to try to create an association between Harding and a sport most Americans followed: baseball. There had always been a connection between baseball and politics. To have politicians present at baseball games was nothing new. But what would happen, thought Lasker, if a politician not only showed up at a baseball game but actually played? The public relations bonanza he estimated would be priceless, and the golf episode would appear on the political goof meter as an insignificant blip.

On the surface there would seem to be a number of problems inherent in pulling off a stunt like this, and all of them with the potential of making the whole thing impossible to do. For starters there was the problem of finding two major league ball clubs willing to participate in such an exhibition. There was also the cost involved in staging such an event. But perhaps the most intimidating problem was making it all look natural, and not some heavy-handed GOP attempt to manipulate the national pastime into a media event for the sake of a few votes. Any one of those problems would have been enough to deter most people, but Albert Lasker wasn't like most people. In fact, in this situation he had either at his fingertips or within his reach the answers to those problems. He knew that one of the teams who could participate in the event was the Chicago Cubs because at the time he was a part owner of the franchise. He shared control of the team with meat packer Ogden Armour and gum maker William Wrigley Jr.[38] Wrigley was also a Harding supporter, though not connected with the campaign, which gave Lasker the perfect smokescreen behind which to orchestrate the entire event. He could pull this off without leaving any RNC fingerprints. In a memo to Judson Welliver, he outlined the entire plan, starting with why the game should be played in the first place. Any announcement of the event should include the reference to Wrigley's recent visit with Harding, during which the senator "expressed his love for the game, and how much he missed it while staying in Marion."[39] Upon returning to Chicago, Wrigley passed the story to Cubs President William Veeck, who arranged for the team to make the midseason, off-schedule trip. The Cubs would be wrapping up a homestand on August 31 and would be heading east for games against the Pittsburgh Pirates and the Brooklyn Dodgers.[40] Getting another major league team to play was a problem, but with Lasker's baseball connections, he had a better chance than anyone of making it happen. He almost got the New York Giants to appear, but at the last moment Giants manager John McGraw complained about the political implications of the event and the team's owners backed out.[41] Lasker then tried his luck with the two major league teams based in Ohio, but both the Cleveland Indians and the Cincinnati Reds turned him down. Surprisingly this piece of the puzzle was to be found in Marion, Harding's hometown. Marion, it turned out, also happened to be the home of the Kerrigan Tailors, a minor league team affiliated with the Ohio State League.[42] In a sense the Tailors presented partial answers to two of Lasker's problems. It would cost nothing to transport the team to the game. In point of fact, cost was never really an issue, because Lasker and the other Cubs officials wound up paying for just about everything.[43] However, having the Tailors play certainly fit in with Lasker's strategy, as outlined in another memo to Judson Welliver: "It [the game] should ostensibly be paid for by the citizens of Marion, who realizing the Senator's love for baseball, paid for same."[44] The appearance of local participation would give the impression the event was a homegrown affair, a natural and sincere expression of a town's love for and appreciation of its favorite son. If the truth ever got out, Democrats might call for an investigation of the alleged collusion between professional baseball and the Republican Party. Fortunately for all concerned, no such investigation was ever conducted. Major league baseball was then governed by a commission staffed by team owners who could be less than partial to any sort of investigation if their own clubs were involved. It was Lasker, while still part owner of the Cubs, who set into motion a plan to put baseball's supervision into the hands of a commissioner independent of team owners. In fact the first commissioner was Judge Kenesaw Mountain Landis, a judge on the federal bench in Chicago and a Lasker acquaintance.[45]

Lasker had apparently thought of just about everything in an attempt to sell

Warren Harding's love of baseball over golf. He just hoped it would be handled correctly. He wrote to Welliver: "Just dish it [the publicity] out as you deem best. The game would give our candidate an opportunity to come out in the wholehearted way he feels in connection with this great American sport, which we believe will be very favorably received by the country and certainly would not hurt baseball."[46]

On September 2, 1920, the Chicago Cubs and the Kerrigan Tailors took the field at Marion's Lincoln Park. The Cubs won the game by the score of 3–1, though it was doubtful anyone really cared. What people and the press came to see was possibly the next president of the United States take part in the national pastime. Suited up in a Cubs uniform and taking the mound that day, Harding started the first inning, threw three pitches, and then left in favor of Cubs ace Grover Cleveland Alexander, who finished the game and clinched the victory. But Harding's on field performance wasn't over yet. Before heading for the dugout, and with the movie cameras still rolling, he took time out to talk about "team play." He accused Woodrow Wilson and the Democratic Party of trying to "go it alone" during the Versailles Peace Conference, without seeking adequate Republican assistance: "You can't win a ballgame with a one-man team. I am opposing one-man play for the nation. The national team now playing for the United States played loosely, and muffed disappointingly, the more domestic affairs, and then struck out at Paris. The contending team tried a squeeze play, and expected to secure six to one against the United States. But the American Senate was ready with the ball at the plate, and we are still flying our pennant which we won at home and held respected against the world. Hail to the team play of America!"[47]

The photo opportunity and the speech were both advertising triumphs. Now when moviegoers saw Harding on the silver screen, they saw him toeing the rubber instead of teeing off. It helped the GOP get back on track with the message that Warren Harding was just an ordinary guy. True, he was busily engaged in serious work. But he wasn't so busy that he couldn't enjoy a sport so many other Americans loved as well. The stunt also underscored the advantages of keeping a candidate at home, where problems could be quickly and effectively handled.

Both the cavalcade of stars and the baseball exhibition were good examples of Lasker's taking what he had learned and perfected in the commercial world and successfully applying it to the political world. Many of the comments Harding made while hosting show business celebrities and later the Chicago Cubs, were reminiscent of Lasker's "reason why" approach: no nonsense, factual reasons why voters should support Republicans and not Democrats. Just like the copy for the Schlitz Beer campaign, or the wording behind the Van Camp's Pork and Beans effort, Harding's message was unmistakably clear—Republicans are better than the Democrats, and here's why.

The inclusion of entertainers and baseball players in Lasker's appeal was also similar to the work he would later do for Lucky Strike cigarettes. In order to convince women that it was permissible to smoke, he would have to convince them that it was socially acceptable. The use of women celebrities made that task easier. Consequently, the appearance of Al Jolson and Lillian Gish, and later pitching ace

Grover Cleveland Alexander, by Harding's side gave the candidate even more credibility with the average voter. Years before it became fashionable to "be like Mike," Albert Lasker was making the case that if you wanted to be like Al, Lillian, or Grover, get on the Harding team.

Finally both stunts had a preemptive quality about them. Once the appearance of show business celebrities and professional baseball players was firmly lodged in the voters' minds as being Harding supporters, it would seem difficult, if not impossible, for the Democrats to mount a similar effort without being seen as copycats. The stunt wouldn't have been nearly as effective, and worse, could have cost them votes if the perception spread that Democrats were so devoid of ideas that the best they could offer was a duplication of a Republican effort. Just as Schlitz Beer trumpeted its use of pure steam to purify its bottles, a practice followed by every brewer but publicized only by Schlitz, efforts to align the Democratic Party with Hollywood and organized baseball would have been relegated to mere also-ran status in each voter's thinking. The Republican presidential campaign of 1920 was running rings around the Democrats in terms of winning voter support, and Harding, thanks to Lasker, didn't have to break a sweat or even leave the porch.

NOTES

1. Bagby, 124.
2. Harding to John Works, 2 July 1920, Warren Harding Papers, Box 505, Folder 4010-2, No. 233330, Ohio Historical Society, Columbus.
3. Samuel Hopkins Adams, *Incredible Era: The Life and Times of Warren Gamaliel Harding* (New York: Octagon Books, 1979; reprint, Boston: Houghton Mifflin, 1939), 170.
4. Murray, 52.
5. Randolph C. Downes, *The Rise of Warren Gamaliel Harding, 1865–1920* (Columbus: Ohio State University Press, 1970), 460.
6. Ibid., 50.
7. Bagby, 125.
8. Downes, 428. Robert Murray, in his work *The Harding Era,* reports that many senators, fearful that their participation in Harding's campaign would reinforce public perception they had rigged Harding's nomination, stayed away from Marion unless specifically asked to do something.
9. Bagby, 125.
10. Donald R. McCoy, "The Election of 1920," in Arthur M. Schlesinger and Fred L. Israel, eds., *History of American Presidential Elections: 1789–1968* vol. II (New York: McGraw-Hill, 1971), 2371.
11. Downes, 463.
12. Ibid., 476.
13. James E. Pollard, *The Presidents and the Press* (New York: Macmillan, 1947), 700–701.
14. Albert Lasker to Will Hays, 18 August 1920, Will Hays Papers, Indiana State Library. The Hays Papers for 1920 are not boxed and are indexed only as to date. Future references to this collection will include the dates and correspondents.
15. Downes, 475.
16. Murray, 51.
17. Andrew Sinclair, *The Available Man: The Life behind the Masks of Warren G.*

Harding (New York: Macmillan, 1965), 152.

18. Warren Harding's acceptance speech (copy), Marion, Ohio, 22 July 1920, Will Hays Collection, Indiana State Library, Indianapolis.

19. Lasker, 133a.

20. Richard Joseph Sinclair, "Will Hays, Republican Politician" (Ph.D. diss., Ball State University, 1969), 126.

21. Anthony, 205.

22. Sinclair, 127.

23. Richard E. Hattwick, *Albert D. Lasker* (Macomb: Center for Business and Economic Research, Western Illinois University, 1976), 10.

24. The 1920 presidential election was the first whose results were broadcast over radio. The phonograph played a much bigger role in the Harding campaign. Harding's speeches were recorded, transferred to disc, and sold to raise money.

25. Murray, 51.

26. Downes, 471.

27. Anthony, 220. Anthony reports the celebrity appearance was greatly helped by Florence Harding, who apparently had a hand in helping Lasker pitch the idea to RNC officials. In fact, RNC Chairman Will Hays was so dazzled by the expert use of these show business celebrities that he wired his thanks to Mrs. Harding.

28. See Downes, 473.

29. Al Jolson, "Harding You're the Man for Us" (Words and music copyright 1920 by Al Jolson, New York). The sheet music was located online at the University of South Florida Tampa Campus Library, Special Collections Department, Presidential Items, Warren G. Harding, as part of the Armwood Family Collection: http://www.lib.usf.edu/spccoll/guide/p/pres/p283.html. Adams, 171, attributes a different set of lyrics to this title.

30. Anthony, 220. Anthony also reports that none of the press coverage seemed to mention the visible presence of "flashing silver flasks quickly sipped and stashed away."

31. Frederick E. Schortemeier, *Rededicating America: The Life and Recent Speeches of Warren G. Harding* (Indianapolis: Bobbs-Merrill, 1920), 67–70.

32. Sinclair, 127.

33. Murray, 52.

34. Downes, 474.

35. "Will Boom Harding by Big Advertising," *New York Times,* 28 July 1920, 1.

36. Kenyon to Will Hays, 31 July 1920, Warren Harding Papers, Box 653, Folder 4692-3, No. 299311, Ohio Historical Society, Columbus.

37. Lasker to Fried lander, 7 August 1920, Warren Harding Papers, Box 520, Folder 4137-1, No. 238380, Ohio Historical Society, Columbus.

38. Gunther, 118. Lasker bought the team for $150,000 in 1916 and then got Armour and Wrigley to buy in for $50,000 each.

39. Lasker to Welliver, 19 August 1920, Warren Harding Papers, Box 520, Folder 4137-1, No. 238366, Ohio Historical Society, Columbus.

40. The Baseball Hall of Fame in Cooperstown, New York, was contacted and provided a copy of the Cubs's schedule for 1920. It showed several off days between the end of the home stand on August 31 and their first game with the Pirates on September 3. There would seem to be plenty of time for a brief detour to Marion en route to Pittsburgh.

41. Downes, 472.

42. Ibid.

43. Ibid., 473. Lasker went to great pains to make sure the other Cubs owners were out in front on this issue to avoid any allegations that the RNC was too deeply involved in this event to seem merely coincidental.

44. Lasker to Welliver, 20 August 1920, Warren Harding Papers, Box 520, Folder

4137-1, No. 238363, Ohio Historical Society, Columbus.

45. Gunther, 122.

46. Lasker to Welliver, 20 August 1920, Warren Harding Papers, Box 520, Folder 4137-1, No. 238363, Ohio Historical Society, Columbus. The 1919 Black Sox scandal, in which members of the Chicago White Sox allegedly took bribes to throw the World Series, had tarnished baseball's image. Lasker felt the exhibition in Marion would help the sport as much as it would help Harding. Despite Harding's proclaimed love for baseball, he remained an avid golfer: he continued to play during the campaign, but he did so out of town and out of camera range.

47. Schortemeier, 107–108.

6
Something Borrowed . . .

There was a down side to old-fashioned porch campaigning. The *New Republic* focused on one of those problems in an April 1920 edition when it said that "even a candidate who stuck to the front porch had to spend a lot of time standing on his legs talking about four or five issues."[1] Inevitably one of those issues would be just where Warren Harding stood on the League of Nations. The 1920 campaign featured a contest to see not only who could capture the White House but also who could capture Harding's heart and mind on the League issue. Pro-Leaguers, Reservationists, and Irreconcilables expended great time and energy getting Harding to commit on the subject and were never really sure if they had succeeded. Other issues were also making a front-porch campaign a risky venture. People were getting used to seeing candidates travel across the country in search of votes. William Jennings Bryan had done it in a losing cause in 1896, whereas Teddy Roosevelt had hit the hustings in 1900 and 1904 with better results. William Howard Taft discovered in 1908 that few people had the time, money, or even the desire to visit the nominee's home.[2] Matters were further complicated by problems with transportation and national demographics. When William McKinley staged his front-porch campaign in 1896, sympathetic railroad companies provided lines, cars, and tickets to take voters to his home in Canton, Ohio. Railroads in 1920 were proving not to be as generous. Also 1896 was a time when most voters still lived in the northern, southern and eastern regions of the country. Voters had since spread out. It would be difficult to bring enough of them to see Harding to make a difference, although some six hundred thousand did make the trip between late July and September.[3] Finally changes in the national political landscape were distinguished not only in terms of distance but also in terms of voter diversity. These too combined to question the effectiveness of a front-porch campaign. Many African-Americans had migrated to northern states before and during World War I in search of more work and less persecution. It was a matter of simple statistics that the number of African-American voters in the North had more than doubled by 1920.[4] Would their relocation to Democrat controlled cities have any effect on the balance of power in those states? Just as important was the result of their absence in the South. Would 1920 be the year a GOP presidential candidate carried the region? Many women were also casting first-time ballots for president. Which way would they go? In areas where a candidate couldn't see the people, or the people couldn't see him, he would have to rely on modern publicity to get the job done. It was becoming obvious that because of the nation's size and the diversity of its voters, the final vote in November would not be, according to the *New Republic,* just the "result of direct acquaintance; it is the result of news reports, the advertising, the oratory, the elusive rumors which are the modern substitute for direct acquaintance."[5]

The appearance of this new challenge seemed to call for new solutions, and to the rescue came modern advertising, led by Albert Lasker. Will Hays and the Republican National Committee unleashed Lasker and let him do what he did best, which was to sell by advertising. First he humanized Warren Harding; then he demonized the Democrats by the process of comparison, a classic example of Lasker's use of "reason why" advertising. The first indication that such an assault would be waged on the voters and the Democratic Party came on July 28, 1920, less than a week after Harding received notice of his nomination. A press release issued that day told of the pending inauguration of a mammoth advertising campaign to sell Harding to the country. All possible tools would be used to illustrate Harding's patriotism and dramatize his campaign promise for a "Return to Normalcy."[6] It would be the biggest advertising drive ever launched in a political campaign: "Under the supervision of the head of a Chicago advertising agency, the campaign will utilize all mediums of modern advertising, including billboard posters, newspaper and magazine advertisements and motion pictures."[7]

Republicans in 1920 had come to recognize that politics was not just about policy but also about publicity. In advancing this "salesmanship campaign," the strategy was primary, the candidate secondary.[8] Professional advertising men such as Robert Tucker of Chicago were consulted on how movies could help portray Harding as "a flesh and blood man, a real human person. I can't over-emphasize the value of this particular effort. You know how the eye transfers the picture to the mind, and how the mind is in fact a negative that retains impressions. What you should have is a means of getting these pictures to the mind of the voter . . . and if you can do it, the first thing you know your candidate changes to an interesting if not colorful personality. After all, the Americans . . . like to think of their leaders in a sentimental way."[9]

In the end, it was Lasker, always Lasker. He flooded the country with campaign literature to go along with the newsreels and sound recordings. He assisted the GOP drive to target new voters by helping to create and distribute brochures and pamphlets to every possible voting bloc that might even consider Harding presidential material. Farmers received copies of "A Billion a Year and Twenty Billion in All," an indictment of the Democratic Party's agricultural policies. Farmers in the Midwest and West had deserted the Democrats in 1918, claiming Southerners were getting special pricing treatment from Congress. The GOP wanted that defection to be permanent, or least through 1920. African-Americans received a

publication then entitled "Why The Negro Is a Republican," and "Lynching."
Women voters were treated to a copy of "Why Women Should Vote for Harding."
Something was even prepared for new citizens.[10] Twice a week eight thousand
photographs featuring Harding and his wife were dispatched nationwide.[11] The
images, orchestrated by Lasker, and caught on film, were shots of the candidate
meeting visiting delegations, playing his cornet when a band came calling or
climbing into the front of a train to ride with the engineer when he left Marion late
in the campaign.[12] Lasker also helped increase telephone usage during the campaign. Workshops were established to perfect techniques for telephone conferences, and similar training seminars were established for the five thousand
surrogate speakers hired for the campaign. They were under the supervision of
Harry New, working out of the Chicago campaign headquarters, and included two
thousand women.[13] In fact the women speakers and the messages they carried
played an important role in selling women first on the Republican Party and later
on Harding. Among the early topics were women's role in politics and the
necessity of everyone to vote.[14] Regardless of the topic, or even who was doing the
speaking, the surrogates were under strict orders to conduct a "conversational
campaign." The RNC strategists didn't want any incendiary or elevated rhetoric
out on the stump. Voters, they reasoned, were tired of the wild-eyed campaigning
of the Roosevelt years and the high-brow verbiage of the Wilson days. Keep it soft
and simple. If the surrogates needed a model, do like the candidate did. Harding
rarely mentioned his Democratic opponent James Cox by name and seldom
criticized Woodrow Wilson in public, except to condemn his interest in what
Harding termed "one-man rule." He rejected repeated staff requests to go negative
on Wilson, vowing he would never go into the White House over the broken body
of the current president. Harding was a gentle campaigner. People who saw him
in Marion seemed to like that. So Harding's apostles in the hinterlands were urged
to do likewise.

In addition to all that, election schools, parades, and a motor corps to carry
voters to the polls on election day were also organized. Lasker did everything an
advertising man could do to sell his product. He even created a slogan for the
campaign, a message the *New York Times* said no voter could escape or mistake
its meaning. It would be there, the *Times* said, staring him in the face as he read his
paper at the breakfast table, and again on billboards as he traveled to work.[15] The
slogan, "Let's be done with wiggle and wobble" was not only Lasker's personal
creation (he used the phrase to describe his displeasure with people who vacillated)
but also a testament of how much power he wielded inside the campaign. The
decision to use the slogan was also an example of how willing Lasker was to
bypass established chains of command to get his way. Using his position to gain
access to Harding, Lasker won his approval for use of the slogan and then told his
subordinates that the "candidate will include the thought of the slogan in his
speech, and will make the closing words of his speech thus: 'Let's be done with
Wiggle and Wobble. Steady, America! Let's assure good fortune for all.'"[16] The
speech Lasker was referring to was Harding's August 28, 1920, pronouncement
on the League of Nations. Lasker's hope was that the slogan would help suggest
the hypocrisy of the Democrats, first in promising to keep the nation out of war in

1916, then getting into the conflict the following year, then out in 1918, and into further international disputes, possibly, by joining the League of Nations. Harding did use it in his speech, although the content sent most Irreconcilables clamoring for clarification, especially after they heard Harding float his "association of nations" idea. Nonetheless Harding did use it in his closing: "Let us be done with wiggling and wobbling. Steady, America! Let us assure good fortune for all."[17]

It was a good thing Harding used the quote. Because even while Albert Lasker was courting him to use it and assuring his superiors Harding would use it, he was telling artists and carpenters under his supervision to begin building billboards bearing the quote. Those billboards were scheduled to go up across the country no later than October 1. Harding's use of the "wiggle and wobble" line would make it a clever hook that would be seen over and over as voters drove down the highway. But Lasker was again careful to remove his fingerprints from his manipulative efforts. He told Jud Welliver: "We want it to appear that when the candidate wrote this sentence in his speech, it was merely a passing sentence that he injected, but that it was so forceful that it was spontaneously picked up."[18]

Not everybody appreciated Lasker's creativity or his spontaneity, which was seen by many as thinly veiled end-runs around established channels. Republican National Committee Chairman Hays suddenly found himself in the middle of an apparent power struggle between his chief ad man and the New York publicity office, which opposed the use of the slogan. Hays began to do a little wiggling and wobbling of his own. He tried to feel Lasker out on the possibility of dropping the slogan. He quickly found out that he, too, could be out-flanked. For starters Lasker had Harding's promise to use the slogan in his August 28th speech, but that was just the beginning. As the billboards were being prepared, Lasker sent a note to Hays in early September telling him that Raymond Robins, chairman of the 1916 Progressive Convention and the only true Progressive on the 1920 Republican National Committee, had agreed to use the slogan for the balance of the campaign.[19] Robins's presence in the upper echelons of the RNC was helping to keep Progressives inside the Republican Party. He had also served as an aide to Hays in the months leading up to the Republican convention, helped to draft the party platform, and later contributed extensively to Harding's July 22nd acceptance speech.[20] Hays, whose rise to the top of the RNC was built mainly on his ability to heal intraparty wounds and forge new coalitions, now faced the prospect of having the Republican-Progressive alliance threatened by Lasker and the "wiggle and wobble" slogan spat. Additionally campaign stationery began appearing in the Chicago headquarters bearing a purple stamp reading "no country on earth but ours could survive years of wiggling and wobbling."[21] Finally, in an attempt to end the debate once and for all, Lasker played his last trump card. In yet another note to Hays, he told him that he had contacted the Hearst newspaper chain, and as a result the syndicate was about to launch a cartoon series featuring characters named "Aunt Wobble" and "Uncle Wiggle." The arrangement, worked out between Lasker and Hearst editor Arthur Brisbane, resulted in the placement of the cartoons in such publications as the *Cleveland News* and the *New York Journal*.[22] That announcement coupled with news that the billboards were under construction and that display advertising was scheduled to appear in the *Saturday Evening Post* and the *Literary Digest* probably pushed Hays into Lasker's corner. He had to regain at least the appearance of some control over the advertising effort, which now seemed firmly in the hands of his run-away adman. In a form letter to all Republican workers, Hays urged them to "make every possible use of those lines from Senator Harding's speech of August twenty-eighth: 'Steady America! Let us assure good fortune to all. Let us be done with wiggling and wobbling.'"[23] To close the book on just who was in charge of the execution of advertising and publicity, Hays sent another note instructing that Lasker be shown all the party literature so he could know what to illustrate. "He has evidenced," wrote Hays, "a most keen political insight in some of the advertisements he has prepared."[24]

However, there was another dimension of the front-porch campaign that began to emerge as a liability as time went on, and that was momentum loss. Delegations visited Marion from the end of July until the middle of October. Day in and day out they arrived, accompanied by the ever-present hype generated by Lasker and the Republican National Committee, but after a few weeks the demonstrations began to take on the appearance of a wornout routine. The enthusiasm appeared strained. The events were drawing less and less coverage. Reporters stationed in Marion began to lose interest, and as a result the campaign seemed to be losing steam. Richard Washburn Child, one of Harding's speechwriters as well as a Lasker confidant, worried in a letter to Hays about a real danger of the possibility of an "anti-climax to the porch campaign. Mere frequency of the visiting delegations is even undesirable unless they give us a chance to say big things. Except for a few occasions which have been definitely 'worked up,' I do not think much of the results. The delegation business must not drift. Let's avoid the petty delegations and get big publicity. If we don't, the middle of October will see the campaign, without any fault of the candidate, sag like an old empty hammock."[25]

Half of Child's advice was taken to heart. The front-porch campaign was modified, and fewer delegations were entertained. Instead Harding's handlers decided to hold some "super days," featuring high profile groups that would allow them to further legitimize press coverage and give Harding a chance to say something that was sure to make the newspapers.

Because women voters were a GOP target, Lasker and Child floated the idea of a Women's Day. The Nineteenth Amendment was in the process of consideration by state legislatures, and the party that could claim credit for securing its ratification would stand to reap the rewards in November. To Lasker, who had successfully advertised products to women in the commercial world, it seemed a wonderful opportunity. To Harding, however, it posed problems. His Senate position on Women's Suffrage was to get the issue out of Washington and into the legislatures for ratification, thus avoiding any direct responsibility for its fate. Unfortunately the process had stalled at thirty-five states, one short of ratification. Women activists inside the Republican Party began to pressure Harding to lean on Republican governors of undecided states to push the amendment over the top.[26] But he was afraid of being viewed as a trampler of state's rights as well as a captive of militant women, who were a vocal, but relatively small part of the women's vote. Consequently, any effort to attract the women's vote by holding a rally in Marion would have to assure activist and mainstream women that the GOP was on their side, yet reassure governors of key states that there would be no outside political meddling. It also had to avoid the appearance of being an elitist event. In 1916 a train sponsored by the wives of wealthy Republicans toured the West on behalf of Charles Evans Hughes. The "Billion Dollar Special," supervised by the Woman's National Hughes Committee, cost the GOP $37,000, was an apparent public relations bust, and may have hurt Hughes politically.[27] Whatever the Harding campaign was going to do to advertise the candidate to women voters would have to be low-key, conservative, and middle of the road. "We will," Lasker wrote in a note to Will Hays, "have to do a lot of special work on this."[28]

Only one hundred women received invitations to attend "Women's Day" in Marion. The event was coordinated by Corrine Roosevelt Robinson, Teddy Roosevelt's sister and an RNC Executive Committee member. Meeting the women in Marion would be Harriet Upton, RNC Executive Committee vice-chairman and an Ohio native. "Most of these women," Lasker wrote to Hays, "should not be suffragists, or women who have made their names in politics, but women in business, particularly employers of large numbers of laborers. There should also be women labor union leaders, authors, and college deans."[29] The whole point of Women's Day was to give Harding a chance to be heard on a wide range of social issues and to have those thoughts warmly received by supportive women and reported by an attentive press corps. The last thing he wanted was to have the day dissolve into some kind of media free-for all where Harding would have to compete with militant women for national publicity. Republican leaders, including governors of states weighing the chances of ratifying the Nineteenth Amendment, had been turned off by female militancy. The breaking point came when members of the National Woman's Party had picketed the Republican convention in Chicago.[30] It would also be an effective way to present Florence Harding as something more than just a candidate's spouse; she was as involved in the day-to-day activities of the campaign as her husband. At first Lasker ignored Mrs. Harding on issues concerning campaign tactics, but when he got to know her, he realized he had in her a dimension that would help sell women on Harding.[31] In addition to his other duties, Judson Welliver was required to provide details about Mrs. Harding that potential women voters might find of interest. What, for example, was her favorite color? Blue. The style of hat she preferred? Veiled tricornered. Did she like low or high heels? Low. How did she spend her leisure time? Horseshoes, swimming, bicycling, and Ping-Pong. Women were also told of how Florence Harding had contributed to the success of the *Marion Star,* the newspaper her husband published. Questions about the strength of Harding's marriage or any inquiries about Mrs. Harding's past relationships were also fielded by the Harding campaign. The GOP let anyone who was interested know that the Hardings enjoyed "a domestic happiness" that was worthy of envy.[32]

"Women's Day" came off without a hitch on October 1, despite the fact that Lasker continued to worry about its outcome until the very end. He was so concerned that nothing go wrong, or more importantly, that an uninvited group of suffragettes might try to crash the event that he spent "Women's Day" in Marion "so as to insure that there will be no heckling, and that nothing will go wrong."[33] And nothing did. The invited guests, a conservative but aristocratic group, were met at the Marion train station, treated to lunch and a theatrical performance, and finally paraded up the street to Harding's house to hear his speech on social legislation. The only hitch was Harriet Upton's complaint that her group wasn't allowed to see an advance text of Harding's remarks, whereas they had to submit theirs for prior inspection. In any event the candidate had a rapt audience as he spoke about the protection of motherhood, the "right of wholesome maternity," equal pay for equal work, the eight-hour workday, the extension of the Children's Bureau, and the prevention of lynching.[34] In the end the national press had a story it could run with, the Harding campaign had a story it wanted told, and Albert Lasker had used prominent American women to serve as testimonial props to add more reasons why voters, and especially women voters, should elect Harding in November.

There would be more "super days" in the late stages of the campaign, including "Foreign Voters Day," "First Voters Day," and "Colored Voters Day." That day almost fell apart when the National Association for the Advancement of Colored People (NAACP) injected itself into the event's planning by raising issues such as the equality of restaurant and hotel facilities in Marion.[35] In the end, however, the affair was effectively manipulated by the Republican National Committee to look less like a political gathering and more like a religious pilgrimage to Marion by religious-minded African-Americans. The illusion was further assisted by the Marion Negro Baptist Church, which provided tent accommodations.[36]

Of course a problem implicit in Richard Washburn Child's letter to Hays warning him about the dangers of endless front-porch events was that the press corps in Marion, effectively leashed, muzzled, and manipulated by the Harding campaign, might rouse itself and do some real investigative reporting for a change. The hypnotic trance of the daily front-porch events might just wear off, and reporters might look beyond the front porch and even up the street in search of other news about Harding. It was news the RNC would rather not have broadcast. It seemed that despite Harding's assurances to Republican senators at the Chicago convention that there was nothing in his past that would hurt his chances to win the election, he indeed had a past that might hurt not only his chances but also those of other Republicans in November. That past would prove to be another reason why Lasker thought so little of Harding as a man, and why the Harding campaign needed Lasker's advertising skills so badly.

One part of Harding's private life that Republican Party leaders really wanted hidden from view was the candidate's extramarital affairs. Harding had a succession of affairs throughout his life, including while he was president. One affair was particularly troublesome. The other woman in the story was named Carrie Phillips. She came from a respected and influential family in Marion. She also came with a husband. Harding's long-running affair with Carrie Phillips was one of the poorer kept secrets around Marion, being known by just about everyone except reporters covering the campaign. However, some reporters were beginning to sense something was going on. Kansas editor William Allen White observed on Harding's Notification Day that "every store front in Marion was a giant bloom of red, white and blue; every store but one. And when the reporters asked about it, they heard one of those stories about a primrose path detour from Main Street."[37]

As Marion continued to swell with reporters from across the country who were anxious for news to send back to their editors and on to their readers, it was reasonable to expect that a story of this kind wouldn't stay under wraps for long. The risk of exposure was too great for party leaders, who were intent on winning the support of women in the November election. Lasker was consulted. After all, he had been brought on board to help the RNC humanize Harding, accentuating his down to earth, average, modest, honest, and faithful midwestern background. Infidelity was not one of those qualities. Something would have to be done about Carrie Phillips and her husband Jim. His silent revenge, manifested by his decision not to decorate his building in Marion's business district, was drawing curious looks from the press. Because of the couple's standing in the community, they couldn't just be smuggled out of town in the dead of night without raising flags and suspicions. Hays turned to Lasker and asked him to make the problem known as Jim and Carrie Phillips go away. In his one and only meeting with the couple, the adman turned bagman and offered to pay them a lump sum of $20,000, plus a monthly sum as long as Harding held public office. It was hush money, intended to buy the couple's silence. But Lasker wasn't finished. The longer they stayed in Marion, the greater the chances their secret and his offer would end up in print. He wanted them out of town, and, in fact, out of the country until after the election. Lasker offered them an all-expenses paid trip around the world, provided they left as soon as possible. By the end of the summer Jim and Carrie Phillips had tied up their loose ends in town, closed up their house, and had begun their world tour, starting first in Japan so Jim Phillips could ostensibly study the raw silk trade.[38] It was hoped that once the couple left town, press interest in this and Harding's other alleged liaisons would lose interest and fade into the background. It was too late. The whispers about what Harding did when Mrs. Harding was away became too loud for even the press to ignore, at least privately. The candidate's primrose path detours had become a genial topic for reporters who congregated daily in the bungalow next to Harding's home.[39] However, they rarely got into print. The RNC in general, and Lasker in particular, had done such a good job of winning the hearts and minds of the press that when bad news did come calling during the 1920 presidential campaign, it was generally ignored or given short shrift.[40]

Another problem that plagued the Harding campaign and would require Lasker's advertising skills dealt with charges about Harding's ancestry. According to RNC Chairman Hays, "We had been aware of a false propaganda campaign beginning immediately after his [Harding's] nomination. We paid little attention until the stories began to gain circulation outside Ohio, disseminated through underground channels hard to trace. On October 29 [1920] and on the following day the Cincinnati *Times-Star* exploded the lie, attributing it to the 'underground section of the Democratic campaign,' and tracing Harding's white ancestry."[41]

The smoking gun, as it were, was found less than one hundred miles east of Marion in the college town of Wooster. William Eastbrook Chancellor, a political science professor who had been shadowing Harding since the Chicago convention, had decided to bring the issue to national attention by publishing "an open letter addressed to the men and women of America."[42] According to the rumor, Harding had inherited African-American blood from his ancestors; specifically, his great-grandmother was African-American and his father was a mulatto.⁴³ Inside Ohio the rumor had dogged Harding through all his campaigns, although it had, for the most part, been dismissed by Ohio voters as just that. But to Republican leaders this presented a serious problem that stretched beyond state lines. They remembered in the Carrie Phillips incident how reporters began tracking down reports of Harding's sexual indiscretions, following those leads all across the state. Fortunately Harding never had to confront the charges in public. What if someone got wind of this story and actually printed it? Even though the Democratic National Committee refused to sanction use of the news in the campaign, thousands of pamphlets were being printed and passed around. Woodrow Wilson ordered the Post Office Department in San Francisco to confiscate a quarter of a million of the flyers, but still the word leaked out.⁴⁴ Even Joseph Tumulty, Wilson's private secretary, gloated over how the news would destroy Harding and urged Wilson to let Cox and other Democrats use it. Wilson refused, but Tumulty had raised a valid point. How would voters across the country react? Although it might have been dismissed by residents of Ohio and maybe even some neighboring states, what would happen if news of the story reached the South, where the GOP was trying to win those states in November? Indeed, according to the *New York Times,* which did carry the story, "echoes of the crusade have been heard from Virginia, North Carolina, Tennessee, Georgia, and even as far south as Alabama."⁴⁵ Would white Southerners who were inching their way toward the Republican Party vote Democrat instead if they believed the story? And, finally, how would women respond? With so many of them casting their first presidential vote, there was concern at the RNC that this news would hurt Harding's chances with them.

Again, Lasker was called in to help. With time running out, immediate action was necessary, but not the kind of action he had taken in the Phillips affair. This called for a two-tiered strategy, first to mitigate whatever damage had been done by the story, and then to preempt the chance that anyone might try to exploit it down the road. Schlitz Beer had gotten the jump on the competition by claiming as its own a brewing process used by all in the industry. Lasker would try to preempt any further damage to Harding's image, and along the way try to beat the Democrats to the punch in touting the racial purity of its own presidential candidate. Lasker went to work, preparing elaborate Harding genealogies for the press, and issued the Harding family tree researched by Pennsylvania's Wyoming Historical and Genealogical Society. The Harding family had first settled in Pennsylvania before moving to Ohio. "No family in the state," the Harding campaign would claim, "has a clearer or more honorable record than the Hardings, a blue-eyed stock from New England and Pennsylvania, the finest pioneer blood, Anglo-Saxon, German, Scotch-Irish and Dutch."⁴⁶ Lasker also got some unexpected help in the form of a $25,000 donation to the GOP publicity fund from oilman E. L. Doheny. Doheny, normally a Democrat, instructed that the money be used to take out full-page ads featuring portraits of Harding's parents.⁴⁷ Apparently no explanation accompanied the ads, but in the long run it may not have been important judging by the results of the November election.⁴⁸

The issue of Harding's racial background ultimately became a nonissue not only because of Lasker's efforts but also because of the press's reaction to the story.

The Harding campaign had apparently built up so much goodwill with the Marion press corps that when the story first broke there was considerable concern as to what to do with it. Louis Seibold of the *New York World,* reportedly the first correspondent to call attention to the story, was followed by colleagues who filed thousands of words regarding the rumors and the content of the published circulars.[49] Much of what was filed was never printed, and that which was got the sort of treatment that automatically seemed to call the story's authenticity into question. The Scripps-Howard newspaper chain decided not to go with the story; Robert Scripps called Harding himself and told him not to worry.[50]

Harding eventually got off the porch and on the campaign stump, either to dodge any more close calls or to refocus the campaign. Carrie Phillips and the Harding family tree were both potential public relations time bombs waiting to explode. Getting the candidate out of town and dragging the press with him might keep those bombs from going off until after the election. Harding and his aides feared a tour would produce slighted politicians with whom Harding hadn't consulted, an exhausted candidate, a loss of dignity, and difficulty maintaining control over the publicity the campaign generated. But now the risks of a road tour seemed small when compared with keeping Harding at home and having to answer questions about what he had done. Fortunately, by the time Harding did hit the campaign trail, it seemed his election was all but assured. Lasker had done his job, and now it was time to let the candidate do some advertising of his own. Hays mapped out three campaign trips, designed to take Harding first to the West, and then into some eastern and several key border states. According to an index of Harding's speeches provided by the Ohio Historical Society, it appeared Harding actually made four trips. He visited Pennsylvania, West Virginia, Maryland, and Kentucky in late September; Iowa, Nebraska, and Oklahoma in early October; Kentucky (again), Indiana, Illinois, and Missouri in mid-October, and finally a short hop to Buffalo, New York, on October 20–21.[51] There may even have been five speaking tours, with the fifth one including stops in Minnesota, Wisconsin, and Indiana in early September.[52] However, the Republicans didn't officially begin the presidential campaign until later that month, so it's possible the latter tour was excluded on a technicality. Whether it was three, four, or five trips, they were all tightly choreographed and scripted. Harding's speaking style on the stump featured dignified speeches and what was described at the time as "whirlwind campaigning." Famed for his overblown rhetoric prior to getting the presidential nomination ("bloviating," as it was known), Harding restrained himself in the campaign. "I could make better speeches than these," he told reporters, "but I have to be so careful."[53] In the end it was his handlers and not Harding who were exercising caution; they wanted to make sure it was the Democrats who "wiggled" and "wobbled" on the issues, not their own candidate.

In the 1920 Republican presidential campaign, Lasker dispatched one of Harding's more troublesome mistresses, controlled the spin on the race question, distracted public discussion about Harding's indulgence in elitist sporting activities, and generally helped paint a warm and friendly image of Warren Harding that resonated with the press and the public. He did about as much as any advertiser could do for his client. None of this is taking into account the press releases, billboards, movie newsreels, phonograph recordings, and photo opportunities that he helped produce. Like the good adman that he was, Albert Lasker educated voters by giving them reasons why they should vote for Warren Harding and then helped to close the sale.

NOTES

1. Gil Troy, *See How They Ran: The Changing Role of the Presidential Candidate* (New York: Free Press, 1991), 141.
2. Ibid., 145.
3. Murray, 52.
4. Downes, 53.
5. "Money to Nominate," *New Republic,* 14 April 1920, 198.
6. Troy, 142.
7. "Will Boom Harding by Big Advertising," *New York Times,* 28 July 1920, 1.
8. Ibid.
9. Robert Tucker to Will Hays, 14 June 1920, Will Hays Papers, Indiana State Library, Indianapolis.
10. Murray, 51.
11. Ibid.
12. Anthony, 206.
13. Hays, 265.
14. Ibid.
15. "Will Boom Harding," 1.
16. Albert Lasker to Scott Bone, 18 August 1290, Will Hays Papers, Indiana State Library, Indianapolis.
17. Schortemeier, 97. Robert Murray, in his work *The Harding Era,* argued that Harding's position on the League could be summed up as an embarrassing but expedient straddle. His misdirection on the League was purposeful, he claimed. to keep everyone guessing (and Republicans campaigning) until his election was assured, 54.
18. Lasker to Welliver, 20 August 1920, Harding Papers, Box 520, Folder 4137-1, No. 238363, Ohio Historical Society, Columbus.
19. Lasker to Hays, 3 September 1920, Will Hays Papers, Indiana State Library, Indianapolis.
20. Downes, 439.
21. Ibid., 491.
22. Arthur Brisbane to Albert Lasker, 3 September 1920, Will Hays Papers, Indiana State Library, Indianapolis.
23. Will Hays letter to Republican workers, 18 September 1920, Warren Harding Papers, Box 652, Folder 4692-1, No. 299193, Ohio Historical Society, Columbus.
24. Hays to J. T. Adams, 3 September 1920, Will Hays Papers, Indiana State Library, Indianapolis.
25. Richard Washburn Child to Will Hays, 9 September 1920, Will Hays Papers, Indiana State Library, Indianapolis.
26. Vermont and Connecticut were seen as likely Republican-controlled states where the Nineteenth Amendment would gain passage, but in the end Tennessee put the measure over the top.
27. James K. Pollock Jr., *Party Campaign Funds* (New York: Alfred A. Knopf, 1926), 162.
28. Lasker to Hays, 4 September 1920, Will Hays Papers, Indiana State Library, Indianapolis.

29. Ibid.
30. Downes, 504.
31. Anthony, 205.
32. Downes, 469; Anthony, 205.
33. Lasker to Will Hays, 20 September 1920, Will Hays Papers, Indiana State Library, Indianapolis.
34. Downes, 512.
35. Ibid., 476.
36. Ibid.
37. "The Other Side of Main Street," *Collier's,* 30 July 1921, 15.
38. Russell, 401. According to Carl Anthony, author of *Florence Harding,* Lasker paid the couple from a hush fund raised by Harry Daugherty from some of Harding's wealthier contributors. The group probably included Jake Hamon of Oklahoma and Ned McLean. Jim and Carrie Phillips returned to Marion from Japan in early 1921. She immediately began efforts to win favors and influence from Harding now that he was president. Gestures from the Harding campaign to keep her quiet included the naming of Carrie's son-in-law to a post in the American consular office in Zurich and a job for her brother as a ship inspector. She also asked Harding to appoint her husband minister to Japan, an idea that died in the Senate.
39. Russell, 401.
40. Another issue worrying the GOP was Mrs. Harding's marital record. She was divorced, and GOP leaders worried her failed first marriage would come back to haunt her second husband. The Democrats never raised the issue, probably because their candidate James Cox was also a divorcee, and they feared being tarred by their own brush.
41. Hays, 272.
42. "Wooster Trustees Dismiss Professor," *New York Times,* 30 October 1920, 1.
43. Russell, 372.
44. Ibid., 414.
45. "Wooster Trustees Dismiss Professor," 1.
46. It's difficult to say what impact the issue had on Harding's support in the deep South. Those states all remained in the Democratic column. However, Republicans did gain votes in the border states. Delaware, Maryland, Missouri, Tennessee, and West Virginia went Republican in 1920, whereas only Delaware and West Virginia did so in 1916. For more on the analysis of the southern vote in 1920, see Randolph Downes, *The Rise of Warren Gamaliel Harding, 1865–1920.*
47. Murray, 63.
48. Pollard, 701. Randolph Downes writes in *The Rise of Warren Gamaliel Harding* that Scripps was not as charitable as Pollard claims. Downes cites Samuel Hopkins Adams who claims Scripps actually said, "Tell him [Harding] we don't care whether it's true or not. We won't touch it."
49. Andrea D. Lentz, ed., *The Warren Harding Papers: An Inventory to the Microfilm Edition* (Columbus: Ohio Historical Society, 1970), 276–277.
50. Pollard, 701.
51. Troy, 143.
52. Lentz, 276–277.
53. Troy, 143.

7
The Man with the Best Told Story Wins

Albert Lasker had done a good job in advertising Warren Harding's story to voters, but that's not to say he couldn't have done as well in advertising James Cox either. In some cases Cox's story was just as good as Harding's, and even better, depending on whom you talked to. Both men were from Ohio. Harding lived in Marion, and Cox lived in Dayton. Each had the potential of capturing the state for his party in the November election. Both could also pass themselves off as honest, virtuous, friendly sons of the Midwest. Their careers were also similar. They were both newspaper men: Harding ran the *Marion Star,* and Cox ran the *Dayton Daily News.* Both men had also held public office before running for president: Harding had served in the state legislature before becoming a U.S. senator, and Cox had been in Congress and was also elected governor. Their path to the Presidential nomination was equally tortuous: Harding was nominated by the GOP on the tenth ballot amidst charges that fellow senators had rigged the convention, whereas Cox had to wait until the forty-fourth round before the Democratic Party chose him. He too left the convention with baggage. In order to win support from the Wilson wing of the party, he had to promise to campaign actively for U.S. participation in the League of Nations. In any event, and regardless of the circumstances of their nomination, James Cox and Warren Harding were the first new faces their parties had nominated for President since 1896.[1] There the similarities ended. Their political beliefs were extremely different. Cox had a reputation as a crusader against political corruption and a supporter of liberal causes. He was also seen by organized labor as a political ally, given his support of an eight-hour workday.[2] His Progressive credentials were critical in the 1916 elections because they helped keep him governor of Ohio and Woodrow Wilson, president. In 1920 Cox's record of reform had the potential of luring Republican Progressives, disillusioned by Warren Harding's nomination, into the Democratic Party. In fact Harold Ickes, a leading Progressive, did jump ship and joined the Cox campaign.[3] Harding, on the other hand, even though mildly progressive, tended to side with conservative

Republicans, especially while in the U.S. Senate. He rarely broke ranks, doing so only when it was politically safe for him to do so. Even their campaign styles would be seen as being worlds apart. Harding clung to his front porch in Marion, and Cox hit the campaign trail with a vengeance. He was an incisive campaigner, not afraid to interact with crowds, even when dealing with hecklers. Democrats, however skeptical they were about Cox's chances, were nonetheless pleased with his performance. Even the Hearst newspaper chain, no friend of the Democratic Party, nor of James Cox for that matter, conceded that he "was a very winning personality with a most happy way of handling a crowd."[4]

Cox's chances for victory extended beyond his record and his campaign style. Some auxiliary issues seemed to mitigate in his favor. The United States had played a major role in winning World War I, and the Democratic Party could rightfully claim some of the credit. The country had enjoyed a degree of economic prosperity as a result of the conflict, yet another chance for Democrats to claim credit and promise more of the same with Cox as president.

With all this going for him, why then did James Cox lose to Warren Harding? Seldom had a candidate campaigned so vigorously, spoken so frequently, yet persuaded such a small percentage (only 34.5 percent) of citizens. He became at the time the most badly defeated Democratic presidential candidate since Stephen Douglas, and sustained the worst electoral beating since 1820 when James Monroe scored a 232–1 victory over John Quincy Adams.[5] The story of James Cox was a good one, but the story of Warren Harding, thanks to Albert Lasker, was told better. Such was the message of the magazine *The Independent,* when it proclaimed in its May 22, 1920, edition that "The Man with the Best Story Wins." Implicit in that message was not just the content of the story, but also the way the story was told. It was in the telling of the story that Lasker played such a critical role in advertising Harding and helping to elect him president of the United States.

The dependence on people such as Albert Lasker to influence the outcome of elections seems to have been part of an evolutionary stage in the American political process. In the nineteenth century, elections were decided by a party's ability to deliver as many of its faithful to the polls as possible. The elections were usually hotly contested, emotion-charged affairs, in which leaders hoped to whip their followers into a frenzy and send them off to vote, much like a general might inspire his troops to battle. The "military" approach to politics faded in the late 1800s, and never more so than in 1896. William McKinley's victory caused a shift in the political landscape, eliminating in some cases Southern Republicans and Northern Democrats.[6] This realignment eliminated some regional animosities and seemed to take some of the fire out of politics. Interest waned as a result, as seen in the drop in voter turnout, party membership, and the importance political parties placed on campaign organizations.[7]

Historian Richard Jensen has described the next phase of campaign evolution as a merchandising one. The description is apt, and certainly helps to explain the presence of Lasker and others on the political horizon. Merchandising campaigns relied on appeals directed to voters through the communications media by experts skilled at techniques of mass participation.[8] The military style of campaigns was no longer effective. Besides the low turnouts and the drop in party memberships, the absence of juicy patronage positions hurt any party's ability to build and maintain an army of faithful foot soldiers. The secret of successful politics seemed to be shifting away from preaching to the converted and toward attracting the undecided. Lasker and others like him were now essential because they possessed the skills to run such commercialized campaigns.[9] The first signs of this shift to specialists such as Lasker were seen back in 1896, when the Republican Party decided to change the focus of the presidential campaign from a military one to a merchandising/ educational one. The GOP must have broken some kind of record that year, distributing 200 million pieces of literature to the nation's 15 million voters en route to electing William McKinley.[10]

In many respects the 1920 presidential election was a further indication of the transition in political campaigning from a military to a merchandising one. Cox and the Democratic Party, but mainly Cox, relied on stirring oratory, "fighting speeches" he called them, to galvanize Democrats into action, much the same way a general would exhort his troops prior to battle. Harding and the Republicans, on the other hand, guided by commercial advertisers and Lasker, who was recognized by both Harding and RNC Chairman Will Hays as the campaign's publicity "idea man," engaged in the more modern merchandising campaign. Indeed, to understand Lasker's impact on the 1920 election is also to understand not only why James Cox lost but also why few presidential candidates since 1920 have ever exclusively embraced the military style of campaigning.

In the beginning, however, the Cox campaign had every appearance of looking like a winner. Despite the fact the Democrats meeting in convention in San Francisco took forty-four ballots to nominate him, Cox was popular not only in Ohio, where he was twice elected governor, but also nationally, given his stint in Congress. He had a proven track record as a reformer, could appeal to progressive and independent voters, and was attractive to labor. He wasn't, at the time of the convention, beholden to the Wilson wing of the Democratic Party, and was on good terms with the political bosses in key states such as New York, Illinois, and Indiana. And because he was popular in Ohio, it was expected he would carry that critical state as well. But from the moment he received the nomination, Cox's campaign never seemed to mesh. There were a number of reasons why. Disillusionment with the war, and the decline in the economy were problems beyond Cox's control but certainly hurt his appeal to undecided and independent voters. Another reason was closer to home, and it had to do with the composition of the Democratic Party in 1920. It was an unlikely coalition of factions in perpetual struggle for overall party control. Democrats from the South and West were primarily rural, native born, Protestant, and dry, meaning they supported Prohibition. They were at odds with party members from northern and eastern states, some of whom were foreign born, and many of whom were urban, Catholic, and wet, meaning they opposed Prohibition.[11] Often the factions found themselves within the same party only because of their natural opposition to the Republican Party. Although they couldn't stand what the GOP stood for, they could barely stand the people within their own party. Dissension became even more apparent during the convention, especially when delegates were called upon to nominate a candidate for president and assemble a party platform. If that weren't enough,

Democrats were hobbled by their own "Two-Thirds Rule," which required the presidential nominee to obtain the votes of two out of three convention delegates, unlike the GOP's rule which required only a simple majority.[12]

The numerous ballots it took for James Cox to win the nomination clearly revealed the divisions within the Democratic Party. He had been nominated without the help of the Wilson wing, which hoped the president might try for a third term. However, even with Wilson out of the running, Cox still knew that he couldn't hope to win the election without his help. So, soon after the convention, Cox went to Washington to meet personally with Wilson. At the end of the one-hour meeting Cox told reporters, "What he [Wilson] promised, I shall, if elected, endeavor with all my strength to keep."[13] Cox promised to support a party platform that was influenced largely by Wilson and his supporters. It called for active U.S. participation in the League of Nations. It is ironic that although Harding exasperated Albert Lasker and other supporters by vacillating on the League, Cox and his followers must have felt a similar degree of exasperation given his imprisonment by the issue. In early 1920 Wilson had proclaimed that the November presidential election would be a "solemn referendum" on the League. It was a corner once painted into by Wilson, Cox found impossible to escape. Cox's pro-League commitment turned out to be a liability for him and an opportunity for Lasker. Through the imposition of the League as the one and apparently only definable issue of his campaign, Cox played right into the hands of Lasker, who'd been a long and bitter opponent of any League role for the United States. Despite Republican difficulties in securing harmony in their own ranks on the League of Nations, all Republicans could attack what was known, and the Wilson vision of the League was known. By identifying with the Wilson League, James Cox became the automatic recipient of all animosity formerly reserved for the president.[14] He was also catching heat for the way the Democrats handled the nation's transition from a wartime to peacetime footing, and the decline in the economy, which sent inflation, recession, and unemployment rocketing skyward. All these developments seemed to take their toll of party unity and all-important campaign contributions. So with limited finances, a divided party, an unhappy electorate, a national press corps that seemed to reflect that hostility, and a confrontation with an opponent who wouldn't come off the front porch and engage him on the issues, the Democratic presidential campaign of 1920 all seemed to focus on James Cox.[15] "Cox is everything," wrote reporter Roger Lewis in the October 16 edition of *Collier's* magazine, "manager, producer, leading man, and caption writer." And if he wasn't everything, he was at least nearly everywhere. Rejecting requests from his own party that he mount a front-porch campaign of his own, he and George White, his "official" campaign manager, planned to take his message directly to the voters. Cox would undertake to deliver a series of addresses in which he would consider issues one by one. He declared that by going directly to the voters he hoped to cultivate the image of an energetic and intelligent campaigner. He also hoped that image would play well in comparison to Harding's, who was mounting just barely enough energy to move himself out of his house and onto the front porch. Perhaps by comparing the two different styles, Cox could force Harding off the porch and onto the campaign trail, where he knew Harding was liable to blunder.[16]

If physical endurance were the stuff by which elections were won, Cox should have been president. "There was Cox," wrote Andrew Sinclair, "campaigning all over the lot in a sweat, in his mental shirtsleeves, with his coat off, ringing fire alarms."[17] Starting his campaign in mid-August, he began the first of a series of whirlwind tours. When the campaign had ended, he had stumped in thirty-six states, skipping only Maine, Vermont, and the Deep South. He gave 394 scheduled speeches, an untold number of brief talks, and was seen by nearly 2 million people. One tour alone, which began in mid-September and ended in early October, took him to twenty-four states, during which time he delivered 238 speeches.[18] He concentrated on voters in the Midwest, New York, Montana, California, and Washington.[19] During the campaign he was arrested for speeding, involved in a railway accident, heckled by Will Hays's advance men, and plagued by bouts of fatigue, hoarseness, and his own temper.[20] When heckled, Cox's passion sometimes got the better of him. After Cox responded to hecklers during a speech by calling Harding a "happy hooligan," the *Chicago Tribune* editorialized that the "barroom flavor of his [Cox's] campaign indicated a mind and a character which did not belong in the White House."[21] Cox was also forced to contend with the occasional partisanship of railroad workers as he campaigned by train. Because his schedule was tight and he was constantly on the move, many of Cox's stops and rallies had to be held in rail yards and at train stations. There he had to compete not only with the noise of the bands and the crowds but also with the noise commonly associated with train yard activities. Cox himself said that he could always tell the politics of the man running the nearby switch engine. He was quiet with his locomotive or not, according to his partisanship.[22]

The mere exercise of mounting a traveling campaign seemed to stretch Cox and the Democrats to the limit, especially when it came to stumping in western states. They tried to make the best of the situation, though. The campaign train carried a special boxcar converted into a makeshift print shop in order to provide advance press materials. But even their print shop on rails found it difficult to compete with time zones. Traveling out west put the Cox campaign three hours behind East Coast time, so all press notices had to be sent out during the night, or else they would miss the next day's morning papers and some early afternoon editions as well.[23] Cox and his staff often worked well into the early hours of the morning in order to meet press deadlines. There was little time for him to write speeches, thus many of them were delivered off the cuff. Cox himself later admitted that when he had to draw what he had to say out of thin air, the draft on his physical strength never relaxed.[24]

It seemed that no matter how many speeches Cox made, or how many miles he traveled trying to reach voters, he couldn't out campaign Warren Harding, despite the fact Harding seemed cemented to his front porch in Marion, Ohio. There, according to Andrew Sinclair, Harding campaigned as "a quiet gentleman, who had no beads on his forehead, no dust on his shoes, no red in his eye."[25] Yet while Harding remained a seemingly unmovable object until late in the campaign, the campaign apparatus built around him by the GOP and publicized by Lasker ran rings around the Democrats. The Republican Party recognized early on that the main burden of proof in the campaign rested with the Democrats, so the less

Harding said, the better. The front porch was proving to be an excellent place for Harding to be, saying as little as possible and looking as good as possible while doing it. It seemed a perfectly wonderful way of campaigning for president, and so in keeping with the relaxed, friendly, down-home image that Lasker and the GOP were trying hard to advertise to voters. No high-brow intellectualism, no beads of sweat, and no red eyes. Instead, nostalgia and normalcy—the way things ought to be. Name calling and personal attacks would be out of character for Harding. Maintaining dignity and decorum were important elements of the porch campaign, as well as preserving the candidate's health. The rough and tumble would be left to Lasker and the others. Their advertising would help paint the Democrats in general, and Woodrow Wilson in particular, as innocent-minded, gullible, stubborn, vain, and victims of shrewd foreign statesmen.

Any personal attacks would be handled by Lasker's ads and the army of traveling speakers that Will Hays, Harry New, and the RNC had assembled. The closest Harding ever came to criticizing Wilson personally was when he referred in his speeches to the current president's preference for "one man government." The line seemed to be a guaranteed crowd-pleaser. He also avoided any specific mention of Cox, perhaps for fear that any reference might give his opponent unwarranted publicity.

The overall thrust of Harding's campaign would be to blast the Wilson administration's apparent record of incompetence and extravagance in general, and Cox, Wilson, and the Democrats on the League of Nations issue in particular. Moreover the collapse of the economy in June 1920 also seemed an easy target. The major geographic battlefield of the campaign would be the states west of the Mississippi River, where Republicans would court the votes of the Progressives and independents who backed the Democrats in 1916. The GOP was not going to repeat its mistakes from that campaign by snubbing California voters who could have swung the election for Charles Evans Hughes. The political appeal and the advertising thrust was to stay on message: Republicans, be they Progressive or Old Guard, were to unite. Those not currently inside the GOP tent were given reasons why they should join. James Cox was just a younger, healthier version of Woodrow Wilson. Lasker's advertising sought to tie Cox to Wilson in every possible way. And because Cox himself had hitched his star to Wilson's version of the League of Nations, advertising a negative association wasn't going to be hard for someone such as Lasker to manufacture. Republicans also sought the support of groups nominally within the Democratic orbit but who might be coaxed to jump ship after the way they had been treated by the Wilson administration. The Republicans reached out, via Lasker's publicity machine, to Irish-Americans, angered by Wilson's close wartime ties with Britain, and German-Americans, smarting from the assault on their civil liberties during the war. Equally responsive to the GOP proved to be business and manufacturing interests upset with Democrat policies toward organized labor, and Progressives angered by certain aspects of the Versailles Treaty. Also of interest were, of course, women. These and other groups, targeted by the Republicans and lobbied by Albert Lasker's advertising and publicity, responded not only in November but also frequently throughout the campaign in the form of financial contributions.

Cox, hobbled by a campaign that was short of cash, and prevented from staving off defections because of the ideological restrictions imposed upon him by Woodrow Wilson, was limited in his strategy. The only issues that seemed to work as publicity grabbers were the GOP's publicity machine run by Albert Lasker and the flood of money that seemed to be running it. "I do not subscribe to the idea of selling a candidate," Cox told the readers of the magazine *The Independent* in its October 2, 1920, edition. "I believe in converting voters to the principles and policies enunciated by the platform and the candidates." Cox's running mate, Franklin Roosevelt, suggested that Harding's participation in such a publicity mongering campaign constituted a violation of his clear duty as a candidate. He told the *New York Times* on July 21, 1920, that "photographs and carefully rehearsed moving picture films do not necessarily convey the truth."

It was unclear just which truths were supposed to be conveyed. Given the limitations imposed upon him by Wilson and the Democratic Party, Cox may have been unable to be as truthful as he would have liked about certain issues, and, if Harding and the Republicans chose obfuscation as a vehicle upon which to convey their principles, what of it? The search for "color," for illuminating anecdotes and human interest tidbits, reflected the new premium on entertainment, on grabbing attention. It also reflected the 20th century concern with "personality." Americans began to view these fragments as windows into a candidate's soul.[26] Pictures of Warren Harding working in his newspaper office, going to the polls to vote, playing baseball with the Chicago Cubs, hamming it up with Al Jolson and other celebrities, or just relaxing with Mrs. Harding on their front porch were the windows Albert Lasker helped open. Through those windows voters saw what they believed to be a truthful glimpse of Warren Harding. Granted, the mediums Lasker used to convey the "truthful" Warren Harding were artificial, but they worked.

Frustrated, Cox and the Democrats—but mostly Cox—turned to the money issue. Campaign financing was not a problem for the Republicans, but it was for the Democrats, and Cox tried to convert the problem into some political capital of his own. The Republican presidential campaign seemed to be awash in cash, and the money trail seemed to go all the way back to the primaries. Frank Lowden and Leonard Wood spent what was felt to be obscene sums of money to snag the nomination, but the dividends they reaped from the investment proved to be disastrous. The nearly $2 million Wood spent during the primaries earned him accusations that he was trying to buy the nomination. "Millionaires Back Wood Boom," screamed a headline in the *New York World,* claiming that he had been underwritten to the tune of $6 million.[27] The money spent proved not nearly as much as had been promised, and the underwriters also proved to be smaller than advertised. Wood's major patron was William Procter of Procter and Gamble, who donated about $750,000. The expenditures, although lavish, proved to be above board. Wood spent lots on headquarters facilities and campaign advertising, but nothing that would be later deemed by a Senate investigation as unethical. Nonetheless the impression persisted from the time the primaries began to the day Harding won the nomination that Wood has out to buy what he could not win fairly. Frank Lowden, although spending far less than Leonard Wood, paid even more dearly for his perceived excess. His campaign had to fend off charges it tried to buy the support of two convention delegates from Missouri.[28] Idaho Senator William Borah, who was supporting Hiram Johnson for the GOP nomination, won Senate approval for an investigation of Republican fund-raising activities. Borah told his colleagues that "if there is a contribution coming to the Republican Party, let it be advertised to the world. If it is not advertised, it is a self-evident proposition that we ought not receive it. If it isn't made public, it is a self-evident proposition that those who are giving it have a sinister nature and a sinister purpose in giving it."[29] For a while it was hard to imagine that this was supposed to be a united party getting ready to joust with the Democrats for control of the presidency. The probe discredited Lowden and Wood, and reaped bitter resentment toward Hiram Johnson because one of his supporters blew the whistle in the first place. The adverse publicity made the nomination of Warren Harding all but inevitable, and gave the Democrats an arsenal of ammunition for the fall campaign, which Cox was now attempting to use.

If the Democratic Party was trying to cash in on the GOP's embarrassment of riches, it may have been an attempt to cover up the embarrassment of having virtually no money to spend on its own candidate. Most likely it was because of the divisions within the party and some of Wilson's policies, which were viewed by business as pro labor and responsible in part for the collapse in 1920 of the economy. Whatever the reason, James Cox's campaign was underfunded. Unlike the Republicans, the Democrats had not tuned up their operation prior to the November elections. In fact they had disbanded their fund-raising branch in January 1920 after it had cleared up the $600,000 deficit incurred in reelecting Woodrow Wilson in 1916. Furthermore the Democratic Party seemed to be in a state of disarray after the thumping it took in the 1918 congressional elections.[30] It was demoralized, disorganized, and nearly broke. A stump campaign needed good planning and good financing to be effective. It had to have good publicity, a national headquarters to help coordinate activities, well-funded branch committees, an army of speakers to represent the candidate in his absence, field workers, and a good get-out-the-vote operation on election day.[31] Cox's turned out to be wanting on all counts. What had to be just as disheartening was the halfhearted effort put forth by prominent party members. Woodrow Wilson made just a few statements on the League of Nations issue, and could manage a personal contribution of only $500. The DNC tried to play off of the president's gesture by starting a "Match Wilson" campaign, but it never took off. Other high-profile Democrats such as William Jennings Bryan and Attorney General A. Mitchell Palmer played virtually no role at all in Cox's campaign, and the best Treasury Secretary William Gibbs McAdoo could muster was a $1,000 donation and one 3-week campaign tour. By October 1920 the Cox campaign had been able to raise only $695,000.[32] Democratic fund-raising records do indicate some high rollers did pitch in to help the campaign: Allan Ryan gave $45,000 and Joseph Guffey contributed $21,000.[33] In the end it was clear the Democratic Party was depending mainly on the willingness of just a few wealthy Democrats, mostly Wilson supporters, to make hefty donations. Money was never there on a consistent basis, and the large donations became fewer and farther between as the chances of victory became more remote. In fact campaign contributions were so apparently bad that in mid-

September some DNC officials suggested closing the national headquarters and quitting.[34]

Warren Harding and the Republican Party had no such problems. Will Hays, the RNC chairman, was determined to capitalize on the success of the 1918 congressional elections by electing a Republican president in 1920. It would take money, but it had to come in ways that would keep the party and the president free from obligations to private, wealthy interests.[35] A national ways and means committee was created, which established quotas for cities and states. New York City would be expected to produce $2, million, whereas Chicago, Albert Lasker's hometown, was obligated to raise $750,000.[36] To deflect charges that Harding was in the pocket of special interests, Hays established a three-tiered donation process. First he issued a public appeal for 2 million individual donors to pledge one dollar each. The next step was to invite wealthy donors to be even more generous, but to a limit. Individual contributions would be limited to $2,000: $1,000 before the convention and $1,000 after.[37] Underwriting the expense of the nominating convention gave Hays another opportunity to demonstrate the grassroots support for the GOP. Tiny pasteboard elephants, the symbol of the Republican Party, were distributed nationwide, with space in which to insert loose change. People donated their spare dimes and quarters. The donations ranged from 50 cents to $1.25.[38] Those Republicans who felt the need to give more than the prescribed amount were given yet another outlet under the Hays plan. They could give as much as $5,000 to the Harding campaign, but with one catch: their names and the amount would become part of the public record.[39] It was more than just an effort by the GOP to keep within the spirit of propriety; it was also an attempt to keep within the letter of the law. Campaign finance laws on the books since 1910 required the names of contributors to be published and a copy of the list to be provided to the clerk of the House of Representatives. It complemented existing law prohibiting banks and corporations from donating to campaigns and set the stage for later regulatory action limiting the amount candidates could donate on their own behalf.[40] Much of Hays's plan was patterned after the Red Cross and the Liberty Loan fund-raising drives of World War I. It was designed that way to seem more familiar to the voter and to invoke a favorable reaction.[41]

Democratic fund-raising came nowhere near the results enjoyed by the GOP. W. D. Jamieson mounted an ambitious letter writing campaign to nearly half a million potential donors asking once, twice, and often three times for reluctant givers to support Cox. In the end, however, the letter writing campaign proved so costly that the money coming in barely covered expenses.[42] For the Democrats the money came in as a trickle; for the Republicans it was like a flood. Even Lasker was surprised by just how fast the money was coming in: "It was a well financed campaign. Fred Upham, the treasurer, took care of that. The money really rolled in. If I remember, we collected and spent nine million dollars from the national headquarters alone. If that amount came into national headquarters, one can imagine what the total amount collected must have been when one adds to that sums collected for state, county and local candidates."[43]

Not only could James Cox imagine just how much money the Republicans were collecting, but he could also imagine where it was coming from and what it was intended for. In a campaign where just about every other issue was proving to be a nonstarter for him, he made the GOP war chest an issue almost from the beginning of the campaign. He split his time on the stump between hammering Harding's front-porch campaign and the "corruption fund" organized by Harding and a "Senate Oligarchy" to buy the presidency.[44] He stepped up the attack in late August 1920. The *New York Times* reported on August 27 that while visiting Pittsburgh, Cox charged the GOP fund drive was a "business plot" by those who wanted "the bayonet at the factory door, profiteering at the gates of the farm and the Federal Reserve System an annex to big business." He produced RNC documents listing fund-raising activities in twenty-seven states and fifty-one cities.[45] In September he quantified the amount of the "corruption fund," claiming it to be somewhere between $8 million and $30 million.[46]

The charges caught the eye of the Senate Committee on Privileges and Elections, otherwise known as the Kenyon Committee, which also had been looking into presidential campaign funding. The committee had been given the extra task in June 1920, when William Borah charged that certain Republicans were trying to buy the presidential nomination. The debate over the usefulness of such a committee included a laundry list of individuals, mostly Democrats, who had secured positions of influence as a result of their donations to Wilson's campaign in 1916. They included George Guthrie who gave $1,000 and became ambassador to Japan; Hugh Wallace, whose $10,000 donation earned him the ambassadorship to France; Henry Morgenthau, who gave $30,000 and was awarded the ambassadorship to Turkey; and Charles Crane, who gave $40,000 and became ambassador to China.[47] Nonetheless the money spent by Leonard Wood and Frank Lowden in pursuit of the Republican presidential nomination put the GOP in the cross-hairs of public attention and offered Democrats a perfect chance to paint them as the party of the fat-cats.

RNC Chairman Hays, his chief fund-raiser, William Boyce Thompson, and Treasurer Fred Upham all testified before the Kenyon Committee regarding presidential campaign expenditures. In testimony that would contribute to a 2,000-page report the RNC would submit to the clerk of the House of Representatives, the three outlined how the Republican Party was raising its money and where it was spending it. Upham testified that the GOP budget, finalized on July 1, 1920, called for spending $3 million on the Harding campaign, but that they had gone over budget by about $400,000.[48] Nearly 40 percent of the money raised was going into publicity, something Lasker, who would testify later, had helped to raise and spend. Publicity costs included $70,000 to place ads in the foreign language press, $159,264.74 for billboard ads, $200,000 to send 15 million pictures of Harding to voters across the country, and $300,000 to handle the shipping of campaign literature.[49] Hays also reminded the Kenyon Committee that most of the money was raised through contributions of under $1,000. He had in his hand the names of 30,904 people who had donated money to the Republican Party between December 1918 and August 1920. Of particular interest were the 12,389 people who had contributed since the Republican convention in June. The average amount pledged, he said, was $82.11. Only eight contributors gave more than $1,000.[50] Hays claimed under oath he knew nothing about a quota system, and he denied knowledge of any contributions beyond those received or pledged. However, there may have been some substance to the charges Cox was leveling. After the campaign it was revealed that major oil companies had made contributions to the Republican National Committee in return for future considerations. The oil company donations never came up during Hays's appearance before the Kenyon Committee, and surfaced only after he and other members of the RNC hierarchy, including Lasker, had left the Republican Party.

Even though the Republican Party was outraising and outspending the Democrats by 2–1 and sometimes 3–1, it was still far less than the $30 million figure Cox was throwing out on the campaign trail. In time the issue began to lose impact, although for a while it seemed to breathe some temporary life into Cox's floundering campaign.[51] When the campaign was all over, the RNC reported a deficit of $1.5 million.[52] But the flap did little to improve the Democratic Party's cash-flow problems, which dated back to 1916 when it went into debt reelecting Woodrow Wilson. It went even deeper in the hole in 1918 while trying to retain control of Congress. It had no sooner balanced its books in early 1920 than it found itself again awash in red ink. The San Francisco convention where Cox was nominated turned out to be a colossal money pit, and when it was all over, California Democrats were left holding the bag to the tune of $125,000. The *New York Times* reported that lady Democrats had hit upon a novel way to try to erase the debt. Waist measurement contests were held throughout the city. Each woman participating in the contest paid five cents per inch to have her waist measured. Prizes were given to those contestants with either the largest or smallest waist.[53] But on a more serious note, DNC officials were worried that Cox's charges would offend independent voters, who might think the charges constituted mudslinging.[54] Those same officials became even more concerned when the focus of the Senate probe into presidential campaign financing shifted from the Republicans to their own party. Investigators wanted to know if the Democrats were getting illegal contributions from abroad, or were shaking down federal office holders in violation of the Corrupt Practices Act.[55] The inquiry made DNC officials squirm even more when it was expanded to look into charges that the liquor industry was funneling money to Cox, a Prohibition opponent.[56]

Lasker, deeply involved in the publicity side of the Harding campaign, was also deeply involved in its fund-raising activities. Once he joined the campaign, he brought with him the likes of Ogden Armour and William Wrigley Jr. Wrigley himself speculated on the money issue to RNC operative Ralph Sollitt: "I think Warren Harding will make one of the best Presidents we have ever had. The only thing that worries me is that we don't appear to have any money to advertise this wonderful man to the voters. We have received about as much as I spend every week advertising a penny stick of chewing gum. We should have at least $2,500,000 to do this thing right and we have to get it pretty quick."[57] Lasker himself certainly wasn't shy when it came to putting his money where his convictions were, even though he didn't think much of Harding. Since 1918 he had spent in excess of $65,000 in support of Republican candidates and in opposition to the League of Nations.[58] Then there was the matter of the car he purchased with his own money for use by reporters covering Harding in Marion, and the times he mixed his work for his advertising agency while simultaneously working for Harding. By today's standards some of Lasker's contributions would have been branded as violations of the campaign finance laws by the Federal Election Commission (FEC), but in 1920 all it resulted in was his appearance before a Senate committee. Among other things the committee wanted to know was how Lasker had managed to make a $25,000 anti-League donation. Lasker said he had made out a personal check to RNC Treasurer Fred Upham, intending that it was to be cashed at Lord & Thomas, Lasker's ad agency. But there wasn't much cash on hand at the time, Lasker testified, so he made the check out to a local bank, cashed it, and gave the money to Upham. The conversion of the check into cash dried up some of the paper trail the committee was following. One Senator wanted Lasker to explain his actions. "It's possible," said Lasker, "that Mr. Upham asked for cash. Secondly, I make most of my political contributions in cash. Most politicians like to get it this way."[59] Lasker's seemingly cavalier response and the temporary speculation it raised about sloppy GOP bookkeeping also raised a much larger issue about fund raising in general. Former DNC Chairman Homer Cummings warned "the real trouble with campaigns is not what the National Committee does, but what the independent cooperating organizations which are not under proper control do. The National Committee can't prevent it, but the government should."[60]

Lasker was also grilled about a $5,000 contribution he allegedly made after the election to help wipe out the RNC's debt. He denied the money was his but indicated that if someone were making a contribution to the Republicans and didn't want Democrats to know about it, it was possible that RNC Treasurer Fred Upham listed the contribution under Lasker's name. And so far as Lasker was concerned, it was all right with him.[61]

Lasker the loyal Republican saw nothing wrong with the idea, but to Lasker the advertiser, the idea virtually screamed opportunity. What better political testimonial could you have than that of a Democrat offering money to the Republicans? Just like show business's perceived endorsement of Harding via the pilgrimage to Marion, and baseball's apparent decision to embrace the GOP nominee, the appearance of a Democrat for Harding might influence other Democrats to do the same. It would help to shrink Cox's dwindling army even further, or at the very least cut into his already meager financial resources. All Lasker needed was a Democrat willing to make the gesture, and the right medium in which to portray it.

The medium for the message had been in place for some time. Lasker had already contracted with Arthur Brisbane of the Hearst newspaper chain to produce a cartoon strip to help promote Lasker's "Wiggle and Wobble" slogan. The series, drawn by cartoonist Frederick Burr Opper, featured the exploits of "Aunt Wobble" and "Uncle Wiggle" in a variety of situations designed to poke fun at Woodrow Wilson, James Cox, and the Democratic Party.[62] Will Hays authorized the GOP to show Lasker all the party literature so he could know what to illustrate. Buried in the records was a telegram from a Charles Sumner Bird, who described himself as a businessman and a former Democrat. He wanted to make a $1,000 donation to the GOP so as to help get business out of the clutches of Democratic bunglers.[63]

An illustration portraying Bird's conversion to the Republicans was, according to Lasker, a "ten-strike. It subtly covers the matter of financial subscriptions in such a way that no matter what Cox does to agitate on the subject, or whether you subsequently raise the limit [on campaign contributions] this will fit in by showing the character of the subscriptions we get. Further, Bird having formerly been a Democrat and a free trader, it gives a basis of appeal which will reach everyone."[64] An illustration as well as other layouts began appearing in the *Saturday Evening Post* during September.

The whole affair was yet another demonstration of two commercial advertising techniques that Albert Lasker applied to the political world. The first was the use of the testimonial as an acknowledged staple of the advertising world. He had already used it with entertainers and baseball players on Harding's behalf. Now he had used it to attract rank-and-file Democrats. The advertisement of a Democrat for Harding also had a preemptive dimension. Just as Lasker had helped to silence comments regarding Harding's racial background by publicizing his genealogy, and indirectly challenging Cox and the Democrats to either match it or surpass it in terms of purity, Lasker's publication of a Democrat for Harding may have neutralized yet another issue. Further talk by Cox about the concentration of wealth in the hands of the Republicans would seem foolish, given the fact that some of that wealth might be coming from disillusioned Democrats. Even the *New York Times* concluded on September 6, 1920, that the only real effect of the "debate" was to weary the country. After September Cox seldom mentioned campaign fundraising and focused instead on the League of Nations and the preservation of Progressive programs.[65]

Unable to force Harding off the porch until late in the campaign when it was too late, or to capitalize on the publicity and fund-raising issues because they had been effectively neutralized or preempted by Albert Lasker, James Cox apparently lost his temper and fixed his ire not on the GOP's messages but on Lasker, the primary messenger. After all, Lasker was the force behind the publicity effort, grinding out more photos, more newsreels, more billboards, more magazine ads, and more speeches recorded on phonograph. Cox could barely conceal his contempt for the advertising executive, and years later he shared his wrath with him: "Cox told me years later that during the campaign he hated me more than any person in Republican headquarters. He expressed himself often that I was a very bad, wicked man, and I did very wicked things, for he had been told that certain Republican campaign moves which he believed to be unfair, were fathered by me. David Lawrence, the editor and columnist traveled on Cox's campaign and often told me how he spent time trying to reassure Mr. Cox that I was not the diabolical character Cox had been led to believe I was."[66]

NOTES

1. Edgar Eugene Robinson, *The Presidential Vote, 1896–1932* (Stanford, Calif., Stanford University Press, 1947), 19.

2. Robert J. Brake, "The Porch and the Stump: Campaign Strategies in the 1920 Presidential Election," *Quarterly Journal of Speech* 55 (1969): 256–267.

3. Downes, 445.

4. Bagby, 131.
5. Brake, 256.
6. Robert Westbrook, "Politics as Consumption: Managing the Modern American Election," in *The Culture of Consumption: Critical Essays in American History, 1880–1980*, ed. Richard Wightman Fox and T. J. Jackson Lears (New York: Pantheon Books, 1983), 147.
7. Ibid.
8. Richard Jensen, "Armies, Admen and Crusaders: Types of Presidential Election Campaigns," *History Teacher* 2 (1969): 34.
9. Westbrook, 153.
10. Ibid., 344.
11. Edward Ranson, "A Snarling Roughhouse: The Democratic Convention of 1924," *History Today* 7 (1994): 27. Cox found himself in trouble with these factions almost from the beginning. He opposed Prohibition, which put him at odds with Democrats from southern and western states, and he was divorced, which hurt his chances with Catholics.
12. Ibid.
13. Bagby, 127.
14. Murray, 61.
15. Troy, 144.
16. Brake, 260.
17. Sinclair, 164.
18. Brake, 261–266.
19. Bagby, 129.
20. Ibid.
21. Troy, 144.
22. Brake, 267.
23. Ibid.
24. Ibid.
25. Sinclair, 164.
26. Troy, 146.
27. Bagby, 52.
28. Ibid., 53.
29. "Debate on the Adoption of Senate Resolution 357, Directing the Committee on Privileges and Elections to Investigate the Campaign Expenses of Various Presidential Candidates in All Political Parties," *The Congressional Record, 65th Congress, Vol. 59* (Washington, D.C.: Government Printing Office, 5 June 1920), 8637–8643.
30. Donald R. McCoy, "The Election of 1920," in *History of American Presidential Elections: 1789–1968*, ed. Arthur M. Schlesinger and Fred Israel (New York: McGraw-Hill, 1971), 2373.
31. Pollock, 145.
32. Ibid., 130.
33. Pollock, 128.
34. Brake, 264.
35. Hays, 256.
36. *Presidential Campaign Expenses: Hearing before a Subcommittee on Privileges and Elections, United States Senate, Sixty-Sixth Congress, Second Session, Part 8, William Kenyon, Chairman* (Washington, D.C.: Government Printing Office, 1920), 1073 (hereafter cited as Kenyon Hearings).
37. Pollock, 71–73.
38. Ibid., 256.
39. Hays, 257.

40. Pollock, 181–182. Violations of the laws could result in a variety of penalties. According to Pollock banks and corporations convicted of violating the 1907 act barring political contributions faced a fine of up to $5,000. Persons representing a bank or a corporation found in violation of the same law faced a $1,250 fine and a year in jail.

41. Ibid., 71–73.

42. Louise Overacker, *Money in Elections* (New York: Macmillan, 1932), 115. For more on Jamieson's fund-raising activities, see the Kenyon Hearings, 1545–1598.

43. Lasker, 133a.

44. Bagby, 128–129.

45. Kenyon Hearings, 1074.

46. Brake, 262.

47. "Debate on the Adoption of Senate Resolution 357," 8637–8643.

48. Bagby, 130.

49. Kenyon Hearings, vol. 2, 1083–1116.

50. Hays, 275. For more on the RNC's fund-raising activities, see Will Hays's testimony before the Kenyon Committee, 1083–1116. James K. Pollock Jr. reports that during the 1920s the GOP attracted donations from sixty thousand people. Although it was a far cry from Will Hays's dream of 2 million donors, it was certainly better than 1916, when the Republicans could muster only thirty-four thousand contributors, or in 1912, the year Progressives bolted the party, when the donor rolls listed only twenty-six hundred. Pollock explains these figures in greater detail in *Party Campaign Funds,* 140-141.

51. Brake, 262.

52. "Hays Makes Report of Harding Victory to RNC," *New York Times,* 4 March 1921, 4.

53. "San Francisco Donates $125,000 to Cover Costs of Democratic Convention," *New York Times,* 29 September 1920, 4.

54. Bagby, 133.

55. Ibid. Bagby reported that Britain was the nation under investigation for illegally contributing to the Cox campaign.

56. Hays, 274.

57. William Wrigley Jr. to Ralph Sollitt, 3 August 1920, Will Hays Papers, Indiana State Library, Indianapolis.

58. Gunther, 111.

59. Ibid.

60. Hays, 274.

61. Gunther, 112.

62. Downes, 492.

63. Ibid.

64. Lasker to Hays, 4 September 1920, Will Hays Papers, Indiana State Library, Indianapolis.

65. Brake, 262.

66. Lasker, 135. In his reminiscences Lasker also said that the day after the election Cox called him to ask if they could meet. Lasker agreed, canceling a postelection meeting with Harding scheduled that same day. In later years Cox was a frequent guest at Lasker's home. They were golfing partners, and Lasker always hosted a party celebrating Cox's birthday.

8
November 2, 1920: Closing the Sale

Election day, November 2, 1920, was cold and cloudy in Marion. At around 10:00 A.M. Warren and Florence Harding were driven to a neighbor's house whose garage had been turned into a temporary voting booth.[1] There, in the glare of the lights needed for the movie cameras, Harding and his wife cast their votes. After that he was off for a round of golf with campaign manager Harry Daugherty at a country club in Columbus. Golf was still a touchy political issue, so the outing was done as secretly as possible. He returned to Marion late in the afternoon to find that his house and those of his neighbors had been turned into a miniature campaign headquarters. Telephone and telegraph wires had just been installed in the kitchen of his neighbor's house where the election returns would be tabulated and assessed. Another line put Harding in direct contact with Will Hays's New York office.[2] As the day wore on, a handful of people who had been invited to spend the evening with Harding as the results poured in, began to arrive. Among them was Albert Lasker.[3] Election day was also Harding's fifty-fifth birthday, so the serious business of counting votes temporarily gave way to an impromptu party, but all indications seemed to point to an even bigger party later that night.[4]

Those indicators had been recognized early in the campaign. The GOP outposts around the nation began reporting as early as September that the country seemed to be heading for Harding in a big way. The election in Maine must have been a sign. Held in September, Republicans won with 69 percent of the vote.[5] But the important news was coming from west of the Mississippi River, where Republicans had set out to win back the Progressive and independent voters of the western and mountain states. Campaign operative E. Mont Reilly reported from Kansas City that "everything in the West is looking its finest."[6] Specific reports from Elmer Dover and Charles Forbes seemed to confirm Reilly's analysis. Dover, reporting from San Francisco, told Harding, "We will carry all of the West. . . . I have never participated in a campaign where there has been as little opposition to the top of the ticket."[7] Forbes, charged with surveying the situation in the Northwest, wired

Harding: "You will make a sweeping victory."[8] By mid-October *The Literary Digest* and other periodicals all indicated overwhelming popular support for Harding. Even Wall Street seemed to agree with the preelection indicators; odds makers in the financial district made Harding a seven to one favorite, in spite of rumors that Cox's supporters were trying to get ten to one odds.[9]

Despite the news of impending disaster, the Democratic presidential ticket continued to predict victory. Franklin Roosevelt told the *Dayton Daily News* on October 20, 1920, that the "silent vote would assure Cox a victory and that men and women everywhere were ready to come out and openly show the result of their silent thought." Party Chairman George White also promised victory, and further predicted that Harding's home state of Ohio and Will Hays's home state of Indiana would land in the Democratic column.[10] But behind the smiles and the public statements, Democratic leaders were already conceding defeat, albeit privately. Author Mark Sullivan wrote to a confidant: "Quite candidly, speaking to you as a Democrat, my judgement at this moment is strongly to the effect that Cox is going to fail in such a degree as to be almost unique in recent elections."

Ultimately it would be up to the newspapers, the movie newsreels, and KDKA radio (for those people in Pittsburgh with receivers) to report just how unique Cox's failure would be. Even the press had a hard time describing the magnitude of the outcome. "Indiana Swept by Republicans," "Illinois Trebles Republican Vote," and "New Jersey by 200,000" were just a few of the headlines appearing in newspapers the day after the election.[11] The *New York Times* was a little less excitable with its rendering of the results, reporting that Harding won 404 out of 531 electoral votes and 60.3 percent of the popular vote, the highest yet recorded in American political history.

A total of 26,748,224 Americans had voted, and over 16 million of them went for Harding. Cox got a little over 9 million, and Socialist Eugene Debs, who campaigned from the Atlanta Penitentiary where he was serving time for antiwar activities, picked up 941,827.[12] The numerical turnout for Cox was almost identical to what Wilson got in 1916 (Cox actually outpolled Wilson, but only by around 13,000 votes), but Harding nearly doubled what Charles Evans Hughes received.[13] Harding also proved to have some very wide coattails. Republicans now controlled the House of Representatives by a 303–131 margin. They also held on to every Senate seat up for reelection while knocking off ten Democrats to increase their majority to twenty-two.[14]

The Democratic Party argued that the way the GOP ran its campaign produced an election of Harding that was more negative in its endorsement than positive. The DNC presented as its proof low voter turnout numbers, and although it's true that less than half the eligible voters showed up on November 2, there appears to be evidence to the contrary. The passage of the Nineteenth Amendment added 9.5 million new voters to the rolls, making the number of eligible voters the highest of any previous presidential election.[15] Not all women chose to vote this time around, but those who did showed a preference for Harding. Some voters, regardless of gender, chose to stay home because they thought Harding's victory was a foregone conclusion. Although it would be hard to classify the no-shows as either Democrats or Republicans, normal voting behavior would seem to indicate that apathy hurts most the party that appears to be in the lead.[16]

The fact remains that Harding's victory was huge, regardless of the turnout. He carried thirty-seven of the forty-eight states, failing only in the South.[17] The GOP assumed it would be solidly Democratic anyway and spent very little of its time or the candidate's energy there. Tennessee proved to be the exception, voting for a Republican president for the first time since 1872.[18] Even if the South had remained solid for James Cox and the Democrats, it's doubtful the outcome would have been any different. Two-thirds of the national vote were cast in the East and the Midwest, and the turnout in those eleven states was higher than the combined output of the twenty-seven states comprising the South and the West. Other striking developments were noted: Boston went Republican for only the second time in its history, and New York gave the GOP a then-unheard of plurality of more than one million votes. In the process the popular Al Smith was swept from office.[19] But for the Republican Party, the real target was west of the Mississippi River. These were areas where Harding never campaigned personally, relying on Albert Lasker's publicity machine. And Lasker came through. Washington, Oregon, California, Montana, Idaho, Wyoming, Colorado, New Mexico, Arizona, and Utah all went to Harding. The news was just as bad for Democrats further down the ticket. They lost every county they had carried in the Pacific states (Washington, Oregon, and California) in 1916, and retained only 13 of the 223 counties held in Montana, Idaho, Wyoming, Colorado, New Mexico, Arizona, Utah, and Nevada. The only two states where Democrats didn't lose counties were South Carolina and Mississippi.[20] Nationally the Republicans carried 1,946 counties out of a possible 3,042.[21]

The Democratic Party in 1920 could at least take comfort in the fact that it had not been completely obliterated by the Harding landslide. James Cox had won 34.5 percent of the vote, so the Democratic Party was still a force to be reckoned with. However, the party's base was much smaller than it had been in 1916. It was in command of only eleven states, all of them southern or bordering southern states, and had garnered the lowest electoral vote since 1904. The Mountain, Western, and Pacific state coalition Woodrow Wilson had put together in 1916 lay in ruins. Many Progressive, independent, and hyphenated Americans who had voted Democrat four years earlier, were in the Republican camp in 1920. Republican gains among German-Americans, Austrian-Americans, Irish-Americans, and Italian-Americans were striking.[22] Democrats also failed in the battle for the hearts and minds of women voters.

Overall the outcome seemed to be not only a repudiation of Cox, Wilson, and Democrat policies, including the League of Nations, but also of the military style of campaigning. James Cox had covered 22,000 miles in the campaign, including an 18,000-mile marathon that yielded him not a single electoral vote.[23] If the strategy behind his odyssey was to galvanize the army of faithful Democrats into action on election day, then the results were less than encouraging. The military style of campaigning had lost to the merchandising campaign Albert Lasker helped to engineer. Early into the campaign, the GOP quit looking at voters as an army and began to consider them as separate parts of a composite picture. Individual appeals were tailored for specific groups: something for farmers, something for immigrants and African-Americans, and, of course, something for women.

Looking at the results geographically as well as demographically, the advertising strategy worked. Farmers in the Midwest, Plains, and Mountain states deserted the Democratic Party in 1920 and voted for the GOP. They had received pamphlets condemning the Democrats' agricultural policies. Immigrants, or hyphenated Americans as they were called then, must also have voted for the GOP in record numbers. They had received publications that focused not only on their general immigrant status but also on their specific ethnicity. They were also invited to spend Foreign Voters' Day in Marion with Harding in mid-September. There they heard an indictment of Democrat policies regarding post–World War I conditions in Europe and Wilson's League plan. Many immigrants, especially German and Italian immigrants, came away from Foreign Voters' Day dissatisfied with the Democrats and showed that dissatisfaction on election day. African-Americans also received special treatment under the Lasker publicity plan. Cities such as Cleveland, Chicago, New York, and Philadelphia had attracted many African-Americans both before and during the war years, and they became important cogs in the GOP's plan to regain control of urban America. Lasker made sure they understood they had a friend in Harding and the Republican Party by sending them pamphlets entitled "Why the Negro Is a Republican," "Even Justice and a Square Deal for All," and "Lynching." An African-American delegation was also invited to visit Harding's home in what must have at the time constituted the most aggressive solicitation African-American voters had ever experienced.[24] And then, of course, there were the women voters. From the top down, Republican organizers seemed to have targeted this group for special attention. Women were listed in GOP brochures as holding important party positions. Florence Harding was more than just a prop in the campaign; she took an active role in the planning and execution. A woman cochaired the RNC's National Ways and Means Committee.[25] Albert Lasker helped to plan and execute at least four separate special events in Marion for women, at which Warren Harding personally addressed issues of importance to them.[26] He also helped prepare and send a number of pamphlets to women. They included "Why Women Should Vote for Harding and Coolidge," and a "New Voters Leaflet." There was also a publication entitled "The Woman Republican," compiled by the Women Members of the Republican National Executive Committee. The flyers, issued to coincide with the passage of the Nineteenth Amendment, hailed the achievement as proof of the GOP's commitment to suffrage and urged women to support Warren Harding.[27]

Regardless of who voted or why, the results were still impressive and got the press and politicians busy trying to figure it all out. "The colossal protest was against Woodrow Wilson and everything that from every conceivable angle might be attached to his name," said the *New York Post*. The *New York World* said voters unleashed on the Democrats "stored up resentment for anything and everything they have found to complain of in the last eight years."[28] Joseph Tumulty, Wilson's private secretary, told the *New York Times* on November 3rd "it [the results] was a landslide, it was an earthquake." Harding speechwriter George Sutherland put a rosier spin on the results. He told the *Times* the same day they were "the most joyous thing that ever happened." A telegram from James Cox to Warren Harding conceded the obvious: Harding was now president-elect. However, Cox foresaw inescapable trouble stemming from the contradictory statements Harding made during the campaign. Cox claimed that during the campaign the only thing he needed to do to prepare for each day on the stump was to read what Harding had said the day before and point out to voters how it contradicted an earlier statement. Summing up his feelings years later, he said, "I thought that the country now knew that as things turned out the joke was not on me but on the country."[29]

For Lasker, the only thing left to say was good-bye. He had done his job. He had sold Warren Harding to the voters, and the results of November 2nd indicated he had successfully closed the sale. It was time to move on, or at least move back to Chicago and Lord & Thomas, his advertising business. "I went to Mr. [Will] Hays and said, 'Now I'm out. I resign. I'm going back to my business.' I never saw the President-elect . . . until next June. He invited me to his inauguration. I didn't go. I was through."[30]

Not quite. Albert Lasker was later appointed chairman of the United States Shipping Board, now called the Maritime Commission, and served until 1923. The Shipping Board was charged with selling off the hundreds of ships built for World War I that were sitting idle. Lasker wasn't the first choice for the job, and the job wasn't Lasker's first choice, either. He wanted to be secretary of commerce, but Harding had already promised the post to Herbert Hoover. The Shipping Board post almost went to Walter Teagle, president of Standard Oil of New Jersey. Teagle had tentatively agreed to take the job on condition that Lasker join him to handle publicity, but when a heart attack felled his company's chairman, Teagle had to remain with the company and decline the government post.

Curiously enough, Lasker and Teagle would again cross paths. Shortly before Lasker resigned his Shipping Board post, Teagle paid him a visit. "Mr. Teagle said, 'I understand the Interior Department is about to close a contract to lease the Teapot Dome Naval Oil Reserve, and all through the [oil] industry it smells. I'm not interested in Teapot Dome. It has no interest whatsoever for Standard Oil of New Jersey. But I do feel that you should tell the President that it smells—that he must not permit it to go through.'"[31] The Teapot Dome affair was the end result of a campaign cost overrun by the GOP. The party ended the 1920 cycle in debt, to the tune of $1.5 million.[32] Between Harding's inauguration in March 1921 and December 1923, months after Harding's death, the debt was mysteriously erased, thanks to contributions made by oilmen E. L. Doheny and Harry Sinclair. Sinclair gave the most.[33] The money was laundered through a number of dummy contributors, possibly to disguise the identity of the original donor. Sinclair's generosity, however, was not limited to the RNC. Interior Secretary Albert Fall was also a beneficiary, although Fall would later claim the money was paid in return for the sale of his New Mexico ranch. In any event, there appeared to be a link between Sinclair's money and the decision by the Interior Department to lease the Teapot Dome oil reserve to his company. A 1928 Senate investigation, in which Lasker would be called to testify, tried to construct a paper trail linking Albert Fall, Harry Sinclair, his money, the Republican National Committee, and Teapot Dome. Important pieces in the puzzle were the RNC's financial records and the testimony of its treasurer, Fred Upham. However, Upham destroyed most of his records prior to his resignation in 1924. His death two years later deprived Senate investigators of a powerful smoking gun.

Armed with what Teagle told him, Lasker went to see Harding at the White House. For the second time in their relationship, Lasker delivered a warning to Harding, this time about his interior secretary and what he was up to. "The President paced up and down in back of his desk as I disclosed the matter to him. He turned to me and said, 'Albert, this isn't the first time that this rumor has come to me, but if Albert Fall isn't an honest man, I'm not fit to be President of the United States.' It showed his great trust in people he believed in—a fatal trust. He had been warned, and still he believed."[34]

Shortly after that meeting in June 1923, Albert Lasker left his post as chairman of the Shipping Board and returned to Chicago. It was the last time he saw Harding alive, though not the last time he would be involved politically. In 1924 he supported Charles Dawes's vice presidential campaign, and Wendell Wilkie's bid for president in 1940, but none of these efforts were as extensive as his labors for Warren Harding and the GOP in 1920, or as significant in building the long-term relationship between politics and commercial advertising.

NOTES

1. Anthony, 235.
2. Murray, 65.
3. Lasker, 134.
4. Murray, 65.
5. Alice V. McGillivray and Richard M. Scammon, *America at the Polls: A Handbook of American Presidential Election Statistics,* vol. 1, *Harding to Eisenhower, 1920–1956* (Washington, D.C.: Congressional Quarterly, 1994), 340.
6. Reilly to Harding, 23 September 1920, Warren Harding Papers, Box 555, Folder 4308-1, No. 253069, Ohio Historical Society, Columbus.
7. Dover to Harding, 9 October 1920, Warren Harding Papers, Box 501, Folder 3991-1, Nos. 231467–68, Ohio Historical Society, Columbus.
8. Forbes to Harding, 12 October 1920, Warren Harding Papers, Box 628, Folder 4555-1, No. 287793, Ohio Historical Society, Columbus.
9. "Odds on Harding Biggest since 1876," *New York Times,* 30 October 1920, 1.
10. "It's Cox, Says White; Harding, Says Hays," *New York Times,* 30 October 1920, 1.
11. Murray, 66.
12. Ibid., 67.
13. Robinson, 21.
14. Murray, 66.
15. Ibid. Murray also wrote that under state laws 17.5 million already had voting rights.
16. Ibid.
17. McGillivray and Scammon, 21.
18. Brake, 263.
19. Bagby, 159.
20. McGillivray and Scammon, 21.
21. Robinson, 21.
22. Bagby, 161.
23. Brake, 266.
24. Murray, 51.

25. Pollock, 75.
26. Lentz, 276–279.
27. "The Woman Republican, 25 August 1920, Published by the Women Members of the Republican National Executive Committee," The Elizabeth Putnam Papers, MC# 360-593f, Vol. 1, Nos. 1–8, Cambridge, Mass.: Schlesinger Library, Radcliffe College.
28. Bagby, 160.
29. James M. Cox, *Journey through My Years* (New York: Simon & Schuster, 1947), 285.
30. Lasker, 135.
31. Ibid., 144.
32. Overacker, 147.
33. Overacker says the total amount Sinclair gave was $260,000 in the form of bonds, some of which were kept to pay legitimate GOP expenses. Others were used as inducements to get other GOP leaders to make contributions. Finally some were used to reward Fall for surrendering Teapot Dome. Both Fall and Sinclair later claimed the bonds represented cash exchanged for the sale of Fall's New Mexico ranch.
34. Lasker, 145.

Epilogue

Surveying the development of propaganda in 1928, Edward Bernays, the father of the public relations industry, lamented the limited impact of modern marketing practices on American electoral politics. "Politics," he observed, "was the first big business in America. Therefore, there is a good deal of irony in the fact that business has learned everything that politics has to offer, but that politics has failed to learn very much from business methods of mass distribution of ideas and products." In particular Bernays bemoaned the fact that politicians failed to grasp the point that their business was about "intensive study of the public, the manufacture of products based on this study, and exhaustive use of every means of reaching the public."[1]

Bernays was at least half right in the expression of his concern. Modern marketing practices seemed to have had a limited effect on the political arena. In fact the principal experts that parties called on prior to World War II were newspaper people who served as press agents. George Creel was an ex-reporter who switched to a career in public relations as a publicity flack for political candidates. Albert Lasker's experience, as we now know, predates Creel's.

Historians have been quick to overlook Lasker's work, preferring instead to focus on such figures as Bruce Barton, Rosser Reeves, or countless others whose contributions were either bracketed by those two or who followed Reeves's pioneering use of television. But the techniques Lasker brought from commercial advertising and applied to politics ("reason why" advertising, testimonials, and preemptive advertising), the mediums he used to convey his message (newspapers, cartoons, pamphlets, film, billboards, phonograph records, and to some degree radio), and the markets he sought to convince (farmers, immigrants, African-Americans, and women) have not been lost on the practitioners of modern political communication. Less than four years after Lasker's experience, advertising executive Bruce Barton wrote to Republican National Committee member George Barr Baker that the "signed testimonial is the best idea that has ever come along."[2]

Lasker helped perfect the use of the testimonial by getting Broadway and Hollywood celebrities to campaign for Warren Harding in 1920. Barton also counseled Baker that "this [the 1924 Calvin Coolidge Presidential campaign] is not party campaigning in the old sense. I have not met anybody who is going to vote for the Republican Party. They are going to vote for Coolidge or against him. Those who are going to vote against him complain that he is cold, lacking in personality and human appeal. Give us an adequate campaign of letters and we will build up a wonderful Coolidge legend in the country."[3]

Lasker was one of the first advertising executives to realize the importance of humanizing political candidates, thereby building an unbreakable bond with the voter. His ability to keep Harding on the front porch as long as he did, and to keep him as newsworthy as he could, helped the candidate project an image of friendliness, neighborliness, and accessibility. His well-documented, leisurely visits with his newspaper employees, and even his exploits on the ballfield with the Chicago Cubs, further reinforced in the voter's mind that here was someone who, despite being possibly the next president of the United States, could also quite possibly be a next-door neighbor, and even a friend. He was pursuing a happy small-town existence, and that seemed to resonate with voters who had grown tired and suspicious of the hectic pace that life had assumed over the last few years. Even his campaign style seemed a relief. There were no frantic charges from one end of the country to the other, and no speeches that overwhelmed audiences. Democrats, by pursuing an opposite course of action, provided a natural opportunity for voters to compare the two candidates. Lasker knew something about comparison advertising; he had used it to favorably position Schlitz Beer and Van Camp's Pork and Beans against their rivals. And, when the Harding campaign found itself temporarily on the ropes, either as the result of James Cox's charges about fundraising improprieties, or by questions regarding Harding's racial background, Lasker was there to preside over damage control. His combination of preemptive and "reason why" advertising in both situations actually put potential inquisitors on the defensive. A modern-day example might be the decision by a candidate to publicize his financial statements and call upon his opponent to do likewise. The gesture both defuses any chance of the information being used against the candidate and puts any delay by the opposition to do likewise in a negative light.

Additionally Lasker's use of market research and segmentation (to get women to use canned pork and beans or later to smoke a particular brand of cigarettes) helped facilitate the GOP's effort to appeal to many different voters. His behavior in this regard is somewhat ironic; he was never a big fan of market research in advertising, preferring instead to rely on what one biographer called his "inspired intuition." Finally his use of sampling in the commercial advertising world dominated in many instances all that is associated with political advertising. Glimpses of a candidate via photo, billboard, or newsreel, and the sound of his voice via the phonograph, and in some cases radio, are nothing really more than samples of a larger product. Like commercial samples (such as cigarettes, which used to be distributed on street corners), political samples are designed to acquaint consumers with a new product and to encourage them to make the purchase when the merchandise becomes available. Responding to Harding's image and speeches as if they were samples, voters bought the entire product when they cashed in their votes on election day. In the process, Albert Lasker proved his worth not only as a packager of candidates but also as a deliverer of customers. It was a concept somewhat ahead of its time, but soon to be seized on and expanded by those who would follow in Lasker's footsteps.

In his essay "Politics as Consumption: Managing the Modern American Election," Robert Westbrook spoke of the "commodification" of modern American electoral politics, a reference to what he called "the packaging and sale of candidates to voter-consumers." Elections in many cases are similar to one-day sales in any retail market. Prior to the sale there is considerable advertising informing consumers about the sale, what might be found, and why those products or services are of such a quality as to make any consideration of a competitor's product unthinkable. Campaigns must create not only the buildup to that one-day sale, otherwise known as the election, but must effectively convey to voter-consumers why their product (the candidate) is superior. To do that requires a certain degree of understanding about who the voter-consumers are. It is not a faceless mass, responding to a uniform appeal. Instead voter-consumers have come to be recognized as a group that arrives at an election-purchase conclusion for different reasons. No one would argue that the results of the 1920 presidential election were not at least partly due to the packaging of Warren Harding and the effective use of this packaging to compare him favorably with James Cox to voter-consumers, regardless of their background. It should be by now abundantly clear that Albert Lasker was as responsible as anyone for making that possible. He devised a commercial marketing campaign that advertised Warren Harding in a way that would more effectively appeal to voters than anything the Democratic Party could hope to do for James Cox. Generations later Rosser Reeves would deliver this blunt assessment of the power of commercial advertising on politics: "A man in a voting booth hesitates between two levers as if he were pausing between competing tubes of toothpaste in a drugstore. The brand that has made the highest penetration on his brain will win his choice."[4]

Not long after Reeves's pronouncement, advertising agencies began to leave the field of political advertising. Many claimed political advertising was merely a sideline affair, and a poorly paying one to boot. Filling the vacuum left by the agencies were professional political consultants, who could offer a more comprehensive array of campaign services. With the addition of these specialists, American electoral politics had finally reached a par with business. The institution had become one in which not only candidates were packaged and sold but also voters. They, too, would be packaged, sold, and delivered to candidates as part of the most significant commodity form of the mass communications industry, the audience.

Today, years after the 1920 presidential election, and despite numerous changes in technology affecting the way messages are delivered to voters, the way those messages are packaged has not changed very much since Lasker convinced the political world it could prosper from the experience of the commercial world. It might have been one of the most important selling jobs ever done, and Albert Lasker deserves credit for closing the sale.

NOTES

1. Fox and Lears, 145.
2. Bruce Barton to George Barr Baker, 26 August 1924, Bruce Barton Papers, Box 16, Folder 7, No. 24, Madison: Wisconsin State Historical Society Mass Communication Division.
3. Ibid.
4. Westbrook, 155.

References

CITED LITERATURE

Archival Materials

Barton, Bruce. Papers. Mass Communications Division. Wisconsin State Historical Society, Madison, Wis.
Gunther, John. Papers. Special Collections. Joseph Regenstein Library. University of Chicago.
Harding, Warren. Papers. Special Collections. Ohio Historical Society, Columbus, Oh.
Hays, Will. Papers. Special Collections. Indiana State Library, Indianapolis, Ind.
Lasker, Albert D. "Reminiscences." Oral History Project. Columbia University, New York, N.Y.
Lord & Thomas Advertising. Samples. Mass Communications Division. Wisconsin State Historical Society, Madison, Wis.
National Baseball Hall of Fame. Reference Division. Cooperstown, N.Y.
Putnam, Elizabeth. Papers. Schlesinger Library. Radcliffe College, Cambridge, Mass.
Sixty-Fifth Congress of the United States. The Congressional Record, Vol. 59. Washington, D.C.: Government Printing Office, 5 June 1920.
U.S. Senate. "Presidential Campaign Expenses: Hearing before a Subcommittee of the Committee on Privileges and Elections, Sixty-Sixth Congress, Second Session, Part 8." Washington, D.C.: Government Printing Office, 1920.

Dissertation

Alderfer, Harold F. "The Personality and Politics of Warren G. Harding." Ph.D. diss., Syracuse University, 1928.
Sinclair, Richard Joseph. "Will Hays, Republican Politician." Ph.D. diss., Ball State University, 1969.

Primary Sources

Cone, Fairfax. *With All Its Faults: A Candid Account of Forty Years in Advertising.* Boston: Little, Brown, 1969.
Hays, Will H. *The Memoirs of Will H. Hays.* Garden City, N.Y.: Doubleday Press, 1955.
Hopkins, Claude C. *My Life in Advertising.* Chicago: Advertising Publications, 1966.
———. *Scientific Advertising.* Chicago: Advertising Publications, 1966.
Ickes, Harold. *The Autobiography of a Curmudgeon.* New York: Reynal & Hitchcock, 1943.

Secondary Sources

Adams, Samuel Hopkins. *Incredible Era: The Life and Times of Warren Gamaliel Harding.* New York: Octagon Press, 1979; reprint, Boston: Houghton Mifflin, 1939.
"Adopt Simple Plan for Inauguration." *New York Times,* 1 March 1921.
"Airplanes Carry Times to Capital." *New York Times,* 5 March 1921.
"All Will Be Well, Declares Harding in Marion Farewell." *New York Times,* 3 March 1921.
Anthony, Carl Sferrazza. *Florence Harding: The First Lady, the Jazz Age, and the Death of America's Most Scandalous President.* New York: William Morrow, 1998.
Bagby, Wesley M. *The Road to Normalcy: The Presidential Campaign and Election of 1920.* Baltimore: Johns Hopkins University Press, 1967.
Bain, Richard C. *Convention Decisions and Voting Records.* Washington, D.C.: Brookings Institution, 1960.
Barck, Oscar Theodore Jr. and Nelson Manfred Blake. *Since 1900: A History of the United States in Our Times.* New York: Macmillan, 1947.
Bishop, Joseph Buckling. *Theodore Roosevelt and His Time, Shown in His Own Letters.* New York: Charles Scribner's Sons, 1920.
Brake, Robert J. "The Porch and the Stump: Campaign Strategies in the 1920 Presidential Election." *Quarterly Journal of Speech* 55 (1969): 256–267.
"Charges Big Fund to Block Wilson." *New York Times,* 29 October 1918.
Clements, Kendrick A. *The Presidency of Woodrow Wilson.* Lawrence: University Press of Kansas, 1992.
"Coast Factions Unite." *New York Times,* 14 April 1918.
Cox, James M. *Journey through My Years.* New York: Simon & Schuster, 1947.
"Democratic Fund Reported: $412,138." *New York Times,* 29 October 1918.
Downes, Randolph C. *The Rise of Warren Gamaliel Harding, 1865–1920.* Columbus: Ohio State University Press, 1970.
"Exit the Old Master." *Time,* 9 June 1952.
"Expect White House Dinners to Be Revived." *New York Times,* 5 March 1921.
"Fair and Cold Weather for Inauguration Day." *New York Times,* 4 March 1921.
Fox, Richard Wightman and T. J. Jackson Lears, eds. *The Culture of Consumption: Critical Essays in American History: 1880–1980.* New York: Pantheon Books, 1983.
Fox, Stephen R. *The Mirror Makers: A History of American Advertising and Its Creators.* New York: William Morrow, 1984.
Gold, Phillip. *Advertising, Politics, and American Culture: From Salesmanship to Therapy.* New York: Paragon House, 1987.
Goldman, Ralph M. *The National Party Chairmen and Committees: Factionalism at the Top.* Armonk, N.Y.: M. E. Sharpe, 1990.
Gould, Lewis L. *Reform and Regulation: American Politics from Roosevelt to Reagan* 2nd ed. New York: Alfred Knopf, 1986.
Gunther, John. *Taken at the Flood: The Story of Albert D. Lasker.* New York: Harper, 1960.

References

"Harding for World Court." *New York Times,* 6 March 1921.
"Harding in Capital: Calls upon Wilson: Plans Completed for Inaugural Today." *New York Times,* 4 March 1921.
"Harding Inaugurated: Declares against New Entanglements: Wilson, Weakened by Illness, Unable to Join in Ceremony." *New York Times,* 5 March 1921.
"Harding's New Cabinet." *New York Times,* 5 March 1921.
Hattwick, Richard E. *Albert D. Lasker.* Macomb: Center for Business and Economic Research, Western Illinois University, 1976.
Hecksher, August. *Woodrow Wilson: A Biography.* New York: Charles Scribner's Sons, 1991.
"'I Say Fight' Is Hays' Reply to Wilson's Appeal." *New York Times,* 28 October 1918.
"It's Cox, Says White; Harding, Says Hays." *New York Times,* 30 October 1920.
Jensen, Richard. "Armies, Admen and Crusaders: Types of Presidential Election Campaigns." *History Teacher* 2 (1969): 34–37.
Laird, Pamela. *Advertising Progress: American Business and the Rise of Consumer Marketing.* Baltimore: Johns Hopkins University Press, 1998.
Lentz, Andrea D., ed. *The Warren Harding Papers: An Inventory to the Microfilm Edition.* Columbus: Ohio Historical Society, 1970.
Link, Arthur, and William M. Leary Jr. "The Election of 1916." In *The History of American Presidential Elections 1789–1968,* vol. 3., ed. Arthur M. Schlesinger Jr. New York: Chelsea House Publishers, in Association with McGraw-Hill, 1971.
Livermore, Seward W. *Politics Is Adjourned: Woodrow Wilson and the War Congress, 1916–1918.* Middletown, Conn.: Wesleyan University Press, 1966.
Longworth, Alice Roosevelt. *Crowded Hours.* New York: Scribner's Sons, 1933.
Margulies, Herbert. *Reconciliation and Revival: James R. Mann and the House Republicans in the Wilson Era.* Westport, Conn.: Greenwood Press, 1996.
Marquette, Arthur F. *Trademarks and Good Will: The Story of the Quaker Oats Company.* New York: McGraw-Hill, 1967.
McCoy, Donald R. "The Election of 1920." In *History of American Presidential Elections: 1789–1968.* Vol. II. Edited by Arthur M. Schlesinger and Fred L. Israel. New York: McGraw-Hill, 1971.
McGillivray, Alice V., and Richard M. Scammon. *America at the Polls: A Handbook of American Presidential Election Statistics.* Vol. 1, *Harding to Eisenhower, 1920–1956.* Washington, D.C.: Congressional Quarterly, 1994.
"Money to Nominate." *New Republic,* 14 April 1920.
Murray, Robert K. *The Harding Era: Warren G. Harding and His Administration.* Minneapolis: University of Minnesota Press, 1969.
Noggle, Burl. *Into the Twenties: The United States from Armistice to Normalcy.* Urbana: University of Illinois Press, 1974.
"Odds on Harding Biggest since 1876." *New York Times,* 30 October 1920.
"The Other Side of Main Street." *Collier's,* 30 July 1921.
Overacker, Louise. *Money in Elections.* New York: Macmillan, 1932.
Pollard, James E. *The Presidents and the Press.* New York: Macmillan, 1947.
Pollock, James K. Jr. *Party Campaign Funds.* New York: Alfred A. Knopf, 1926.
Porter, Glenn. *The Rise of Big Business.* Wheeling, Ill.: Harlan Davidson, 1992.
"Prince of Hucksters." *Time,* 29 August 1960.
Ranson, Edward. "A Snarling Roughhouse: The Democratic Convention of 1924." *History Today* 44 (1994): 24–27.
"Ready for Simple Ceremonies." *New York Times,* 4 March 1921.
Robinson, Edgar Eugene. *The Presidential Vote, 1896–1932.* Stanford, Calif., Stanford University Press, 1947.

Russell, Francis. *The Shadow of Blooming Grove: Warren G. Harding in His Times.* New York: McGraw-Hill, 1968.
Schlesinger, Arthur M. Jr. *The Crisis of the Old Order, 1919–1933.* Boston: Houghton Mifflin, 1956.
Schortemeier, Frederick E. *Rededicating America: The Life and Recent Speeches of Warren G. Harding.* Indianapolis, Ind.: Bobbs-Merrill, 1920.
Sinclair, Andrew. *Prohibition: The Era of Excess.* Boston: Little, Brown and Company, 1962.
———. *The Available Man: The Life Behind the Masks of Warren G. Harding.* New York: Macmillan, 1965.
Sullivan, Mark. *Our Times: America at the Birth of the Twentieth Century.* New York: Charles Scribner's Sons, 1933.
Swanberg, W. A. *Citizen Hearst: A Biography of William Randolph Hearst.* New York: Charles Scribner's Sons, 1961.
"Taft and Roosevelt in Appeal to Voters." *New York Times*, 1 November 1918.
"Text of President Harding's Inaugural Address." *New York Times*, 5 March 1921.
"Text of President Wilson's Appeal." *New York Times*, 26 October 1918.
Trani, Eugene P., and David L. Wilson. *The Presidency of Warren G. Harding.* Lawrence: Regents Press of Kansas, 1977.
Troy, Gil. *See How They Ran: The Changing Role of the Presidential Candidate.* New York: Free Press, 1991.
Westbrook, Robert. "Politics as Consumption: Managing the Modern American Election." In *The Culture of Consumption: Critical Essays in American History, 1880–1980.* Edited by Richard Wightman Fox and T. J. Jackson Lears. New York: Pantheon Books, 1983.
"Will Boom Harding by Big Advertising." *New York Times*, 28 July 1920.
"William Jennings Bryan Speech Read at Test of Inaugural Sound System." *New York Times*, 3 March 1921.
"Wilson Appeals to Nation." *New York Times*, 26 October 1918.
"Wooster Trustees Dismiss Professor." *New York Times*, 30 October 1920.

BIBLIOGRAPHY

Dissertations

Cobb, Lawrence Wells. "Patriotic Themes in American Magazine Advertising, 1898–1945." Ph.D. diss., Emory University, 1978.
Hutchinson, Sara Etta. "The Pioneers of Advertising: A Study of the Relationship of Their Personalities to Their Contributions to Advertising." M.A. thesis, University of Georgia, 1981.

Primary Sources

Cone, Fairfax. *The Blue Streak: Some Observations, Mostly about Advertising.* Chicago: Crain Communications, 1973.
Hart, George. *Official Report of the Proceedings of the Seventeenth Republican National Convention.* New York: Tenney Press, 1920.
Republican National Committee. *Republican National Campaign Textbook, 1920.* Washington, D.C.: Republican National Committee, 1920.

Secondary Sources

ABC Clio Information Services. *The Democratic and Republican Parties in America: A Historical Biography.* Santa Barbara, Calif.: ABC Clio Services, 1980.

References

Archer, Leonard. *The History of Radio to 1926.* New York: Arno Press, 1971.
Atwan, Robert, Donald McQuade, and John Wright. *Easels, Luckies, and Frigidaires: Advertising the American Way.* New York: Dell Publishing, 1979.
Bagby, Wesley M. "The Smoke Filled Room and the Nomination of Warren G. Harding." *Mississippi Valley Historical Review* 4 (March 1955): 175–184.
Barry, Richard. "The Republican Party's Attitude." *New York Times Magazine,* 30 June 1918.
Barton, Bruce. *The Man Nobody Knows: A Discovery of the Real Jesus.* Indianapolis, Ind.: Bobbs-Merrill, 1926.
Bean, Louis. *Ballot Behavior: A Study of Presidential Elections.* Washington, D.C.: American Council on Public Affairs, 1940.
Bernays, Edward. *Crystallizing Public Opinion.* New York: Boni and Liveright, 1920.
———. *Propaganda.* New York: Horace Liveright, 1928.
Bernstein, S. R. *The Lasker Story, as He Told It.* Lincolnwood, Ill.: NTC Business Books, 1963.
Boller, Paul Jr. *Presidential Anecdotes.* New York: Oxford University Press, 1981.
Chapple, Joe Mitchell. *Warren G. Harding: The Man.* Boston: Chapple Publishing, 1962.
Creel, George. *How We Advertised America.* New York: Harper Brothers, 1920.
Diamond, Edwin. "30-Second Elections." *New York Magazine,* 1 October 1984.
Ewen, Stuart. *Captains of Consciousness: Advertising and the Social Roots of the Consumer Culture.* New York: McGraw-Hill, 1976.
Fochs, Arnold. *Advertising That Won Elections.* Duluth, Minn.: A. J. Publishers, 1980.
Fraser, James Howard. *The American Billboard: 100 Years.* New York: Harry N. Abrams, 1991.
Gundlach, E. T. *Facts and Fetishes in Advertising.* Chicago: Consolidated Publishing, 1931.
Hyman, Sydney. *The Lives of William Benton.* Chicago: University of Chicago Press, 1969.
Jamieson, Kathleen Hall. *Packaging the Presidency.* New York: Oxford University Press, 1992.
Jensen, Richard. *The Winning of the Midwest: Social and Political Conflict, 1888–1896.* Chicago: University of Chicago Press, 1971.
Jones, Howard Alfred. *Fifty Years behind the Scenes in Advertising.* Philadelphia: Torrance & Co., 1975.
Laird, Pamela Walker. "From Success to Progress: The Professionalization and Legitimization of Advertising Practitioners, 1820–1920." *Business and Economic History* 21 (1992): 307–316.
Lippincott, Wilmot. *Outdoor Advertising.* New York: McGraw-Hill, 1923.
Lord & Thomas. *The Book of Advertising Tests: A Group of Articles That Actually Say Something about Advertising.* Chicago: University of Illinois Library, 1905.
Marchand, Roland. "The Golden Age of Advertising." *American Heritage Magazine* 36 (April-May 1985): 74–89.
Miles, William. *The Image Makers: A Bibliography of American Presidential Campaign Biographies.* Metuchen, N.J.: Scarecrow Press, 1979.
Mitchell, Greg. "How Media Politics Was Born." *American Heritage Magazine* 39 (September-October 1988): 34–41.
Packard, Vance. *The Hidden Persuaders.* New York: Simon & Schuster, 1957.
Paschal, Jules F. *Mr. Justice Sutherland: A Man against the State.* Princeton: Princeton University Press, 1951.
Presbrey, Frank. *The History and Development of Advertising.* Garden City, N.Y.: Doubleday Press, 1929.
Reeves, Rosser. *Reality in Advertising.* New York: Alfred A. Knopf, 1961.
Roseboom. Eugene H. *A History of Presidential Elections.* New York: Macmillan, 1957.

Spragens, Edward. *Popular Images of American Presidents.* New York: Green Publishers, 1988.
Thomson, Charles Willis. "Campaigning from Porch and Stump." *New York Times Book Review and Magazine,* 1 August 1920.
Watkins, Julian. *The 100 Greatest Advertisements: Who Wrote Them and What They Did.* New York: Moore Publishing, 1949.

Index

Adams, John Quincy, 76
African-American, 2, 63, 70, 71, 94
American Tobacco Company, 21, 22
Amos 'n' Andy Show, 54
Anheuser Busch, 16, 19
Armistice, 5, 6, 13, 105
Armour, Ogden, 16, 34, 35, 57, 60, 85
Ayer, N. W., 17

Baker, George Barr, 99, 102
Barrymore, Ethyl, 54
Barton, Bruce, 27, 99, 100, 102, 103, 107
Baseball, 15, 56-61, 81, 87, 103
Bernays, Edward, 99
Billboards, 6, 55, 65, 66, 73, 87, 99
Blackstone Hotel, 41, 44
Bone, Scott, 39, 51, 73
Borah, William, 82, 84
Boston, 93
Brandegee, Frank, 34, 41, 43, 50
Brisbane, Arthur, 66, 73, 86
Brooklyn Dodgers, 57
Bryan, William Jennings, 13, 28, 63, 82

California, 3, 28, 29, 38, 79, 80, 85, 93
Camels, 21
Campaign finance, 83, 86
Capitol, 5, 9, 10, 12, 38
Chancellor, William Eastbrook, 70

Chesterfields, 21
Chicago, 3, 4, 16, 18-21, 24, 29, 33, 35, 37, 39-42, 44, 45, 47, 51, 54, 61, 64-66, 68-70, 79, 83, 94-96
Chicago Coliseum, 40-42
Chicago Cubs, 15, 57, 58, 81, 100
Chicago Tribune, 79
Child, Richard Washburn, 53, 67, 73
Cincinnati, 38, 56, 57, 70
Cincinnati Reds, 56, 57
Cincinnati Times-Star, 70
Collier's magazine, 78
Colored Voters Day, 69
Columbus, Indiana, 28
Columbus, Ohio, 91
Committee on Public Information, 27
Congress, 1, 5-7, 24, 30-33, 35, 37, 64, 75, 77, 85, 88
Connecticut, 34, 41, 43, 50, 73
Coolidge, Calvin, 10-12, 27, 54, 55, 94, 100
Corbally, Irene, 56
Corrupt Practices Act, 85
Cox, James, 50, 56, 65, 71, 74-89, 92-97, 101
Crane, Charles, 84
Creel, George, 27, 99
Crocker, Will, 34
Cummings, Homer, 86
Curtis, Charles, 41
Curtis, Cyrus, 19

Daugherty, Harry, 8, 12, 38, 50, 74, 91
Davenport, 20
Davis, James, 8
Dayton Daily News, 75, 92
Debs, Eugene, 15, 92
Democratic Party, 1, 28, 32-34, 49, 52, 58, 59, 64, 75-78, 81, 82, 86, 92-94, 101
Denby, Edwin, 8
Doheny, E. L., 71, 95
Dover, Elmer, 91

Eighteenth Amendment, 5

Fall, Albert, 8, 12, 95, 96
Federal Election Commission (FEC), 86
Fess, Simeon, 30
Firestone, Harvey, 40
First Voters Day, 69
Florida, 8, 43, 60
Forbes, Charles, 12, 91
Foreign Relations Committee, 34
Foreign Voters Day, 69
Fourteen Points, 29, 30
Frankfurter, Felix, 39
Front porch, 6, 44, 50-56, 63, 67, 69, 76, 78-81, 84, 100
Fund-raising, 35, 40, 48, 82-85, 87, 89, 100

Galveston Daily News, 28
Gish, Lillian, 54, 58
Golf, 15, 16, 24, 56, 58, 91
Grand Old Party (GOP), 1, 3, 6, 8, 24, 28-34, 37, 42, 43, 46, 50-53, 56, 58, 64, 67, 68, 71, 74, 75, 77, 79, 80, 82-84, 86, 89, 91-97
Guffey, Joseph, 82

Harding, Florence, 13, 54, 60, 68, 74, 91, 94
Harding, Warren, 2-4, 6-15, 27, 38-61, 63-87, 89, 91-96, 100, 101
Hays, Will, 1, 8, 24, 28-35, 37-39, 41, 43, 46-53, 55, 56, 59, 60, 64, 66-70, 72-74, 77, 80, 83, 84, 86, 88, 89, 95, 96
Hearst newspaper chain, 66, 76, 86
Hearst, William Randolph, 46, 48

Hert, Alvin, 43
Hoover, Herbert, 13, 95
Hopkins, Claude, 18-20, 25
Hughes, Charles Evans, 8, 11, 28, 39, 68, 80, 92

Ickes, Harold, 39, 47, 75
Inaugural, 7-14
Inauguration, 3, 7, 9, 10, 13, 64, 95
The Independent, 76, 81, 86
Indiana, 1, 22, 24, 28, 29, 38, 43, 49, 60, 72, 77, 92
Irwin, William G., 24, 28, 29

Johnson, Hiram, 2, 29, 38-45, 47, 82
Jolson, Al, 54, 55, 58, 60, 81

Kansas City, 51, 91
Kennedy, John, 17, 18
Kenyon Committee, 84, 85, 89
Kenyon, William, 56, 88
Kerrigan Tailors, 57, 58
Kimberly Clark, 20
Kleenex, 15
Knox Building, 31
Knox, Philander, 10
Kotex, 15, 20, 21

Ladies' Home Journal, 19, 21, 23
Lake Forest, 16, 24, 47
Lasker, Albert, 1, 2, 4, 7, 8, 13, 15-25, 27-35, 37-43, 45-57, 59-61, 64-81, 83-87, 89, 91, 93-97, 99-101
Lasker, Flora, 21
Lasker, Morris, 16
Lawrence, David, 87
League of Nations, 1, 2, 15, 29, 33-35, 37-42, 44, 46, 49, 63, 65, 66, 75, 78, 80, 82, 85, 87, 93
League to Enforce Peace, 37
Liberty Bond, 54
Liggett & Myers, 21
Liquozone, 19
Literary Digest, 67, 92
Lodge, Henry Cabot, 7, 10, 11, 29, 34, 37, 41-43, 47, 53
Lord & Thomas, 1, 4, 15-24, 31, 46, 54, 86, 95
Lord, Daniel, 16, 17
Lowden, Frank, 39-48, 81, 82, 84

Index

Lucky Strike, 1, 13, 15, 20-22, 37, 58

Marion, 6, 9, 10, 40, 46, 50-61, 65, 67-70, 72, 74-76, 79, 85, 86, 91, 94
Marion Star, 56, 68, 75
Maritime Commission, 95
Marshall, Thomas, 11
McCormick, Medill, 34, 41
McCormick, Ruth, 45
McKinley, William, 9, 44, 50, 63, 77
McLean, Ned, 7, 74
Mellon, Andrew, 8, 11
Metropolitan Opera, 22, 54
Montgomery Ward, 17
Morgenthau, Henry, 84
Motion pictures, 2, 27, 55, 64
Movie, 4, 6, 50, 52, 54-56, 58, 73, 91, 92
Mt. Vernon Avenue, 52

National Association for the Advancement of Colored People (NAACP), 69
National Association of Republican State Chairmen, 45
National Speaker's Bureau, 51
National Woman's Party, 68
New, Harry, 51, 65, 80
New Republic, 63, 64
New York, 7, 9, 13, 14, 22, 24, 25, 29-32, 34, 35, 37, 43, 47, 48, 51, 54, 57, 59, 60, 65, 66, 71-74, 77, 79, 81, 83-85, 87-89, 91-94, 96, 97
New York Giants, 57
New York Journal, 66
New York Post, 47, 94
New York Sun, 51
New York Times, 7, 9, 13, 14, 34, 35, 43, 60, 65, 71, 73, 74, 81, 84, 85, 87, 89, 92, 94, 96
New York World, 72, 81, 94
Nineteenth Amendment, 67, 68, 73, 92, 94

Ohio, 2, 6, 9, 29, 32, 35, 38-40, 44, 45, 47-50, 52, 56, 57, 63, 68, 70-72, 75, 77, 79, 92
Ohio Historical Society, 49, 72
Ohio State League, 57
Oil, 18, 85, 95

Old Guard, 1, 28, 31, 33, 40, 42, 44, 45, 47, 80

Palmer, A. Mitchell, 11, 82
Palmolive, 15
Pennsylvania, 9, 10, 38, 43, 44, 51, 71, 72
Penrose, Boies, 38, 44, 51
Pepsodent, 15, 54
Phillips, Carrie, 69-72, 74
Pittsburgh Pirates, 57
Post, 7, 8, 12, 13, 19, 20, 23, 39, 47, 66, 71, 74, 87, 94-96
Preemptive advertising, 1, 2, 34, 54, 59, 87, 99, 100
Primary, 38, 56
Procter and Gamble, 17, 35, 39, 81
Procter, William, 35, 38, 39, 81
Progressive, 1, 28, 29, 31, 33, 38-40, 45, 47, 66, 75, 77, 80, 87, 91, 93
Progressive Party, 45
Prohibition, 5, 13, 42, 44, 77, 85, 88

Quaker Oats, 15, 20, 25

Radio, 4, 15, 54, 60, 92, 99, 100
Reason why advertising, 1, 15, 17, 18, 20, 22-24, 31, 33, 34, 39, 50, 54, 58, 64, 69, 99, 100
Reilly, E. Mont, 91
Republican National Committee (RNC), 1, 2, 24, 28-33, 37, 39, 41-43, 46-49, 51, 53, 55-57, 60, 64-71, 77, 80, 83-86, 95, 99
Republican Party, 1, 4, 24, 27-34, 37, 38, 41, 42, 44, 45, 48, 49, 52, 53, 57, 65-67, 69, 71, 77, 79, 82-85, 93, 94, 100
Robins, Raymond, 66
Robinson, Corrine Roosevelt, 68
Roosevelt, Alice, 12, 45
Roosevelt, Franklin, 15, 81, 92
Roosevelt, Ted, 12
Roosevelt, Theodore, 9, 28-30, 32, 35, 37-40, 44, 45, 47, 51, 63, 65, 68
Root, Elihu, 41
Russell, Lillian, 54

Saturday Evening Post, 19, 23, 66, 87
Schlitz Beer, 19, 58, 59, 71, 100

Scobey, Ed, 40
Scripps, Robert, 72
Scripps-Howard, 72
Secret Service, 7, 10
Seibold, Louis, 72
Senate, 1, 7, 8, 10, 12, 28-30, 32, 34, 35, 38-40, 42-48, 53, 58, 67, 74, 76, 81, 82, 84-86, 88, 89, 92, 95, 96
Senate Committee on Arrangements, 7, 10
Senate Committee on Privileges and Elections, 84
Shipping Board, 8, 13, 95, 96
Shoreham Hotel, 34
Sinclair, Harry, 95
Smith, Jess, 12
Smoot, Reed, 30, 38, 41
Sollitt, Ralph, 85, 89
Sound recording, 2
Stack, J. L., 19
Standard Oil of New Jersey, 95
Suite 404, 41-43
Sullivan, Mark, 47, 92
Sunkist, 1, 17
Supreme Court, 11, 53
Sutherland, George, 53, 94
Swift Packing Company, 18
Syracuse, 48, 56

Taft, William Howard, 28, 29, 32, 35, 37, 39, 45, 63
Teagle, Walter, 95, 96
Teapot Dome, 95, 97
Testimonial, 2, 22, 54, 69, 86, 87, 99, 100
Thomas, Ambrose, 16, 17
Thompson, Carmi, 40
Thompson, J. Walter, 17, 30
Thompson, William Boyce, 30, 33, 84
Tip Top Inn, 21, 25
Truman, Harry, 15
Tucker, Robert, 64, 73
Tumulty, Joseph, 71, 94

United Nations, 16
United States Shipping Board, 95
Upham, Fred, 51, 83, 84, 86, 95
Upton, Harriet, 68

Van Camp, 1
Veeck, William, 57
Versailles Peace Conference, 58
Versailles Treaty, 80
Victory Way, 52, 54

Wallace, Henry, 8
Wallace, Hugh, 84
Wardman Park Hotel, 44
Washington, D. C., 3, 5-10, 12, 32, 34, 37, 44, 45, 47, 55, 67, 78
Weeks, John, 8
Welliver, Judson, 51, 57, 58, 60, 61, 66, 68, 73
Westbrook, Robert, 88, 101
White, Edward, 11
White, George, 78, 92
White House, 3, 4, 7, 10, 12, 13, 24, 28, 37, 39, 49, 54, 63, 65, 79, 96
White, William Allen, 39, 69
Wiggle, 46, 65, 66, 86
Willard Hotel, 10
Wilson, Woodrow, 3-14, 28-35, 39-42, 50, 53, 58, 65, 71, 75, 77, 78, 80-82, 85, 86, 92-94
Winnetka, 39
Wire photography, 2
Wobble, 46, 65, 66, 86
Woman's Made in America League, 7
Women, 3-5, 7-9, 11, 21-23, 37, 58, 64, 65, 67-71, 80, 92-94, 97, 99, 100
Women's Day, 67, 68
Women's suffrage, 37, 44, 67
World War I, 1, 5-9, 15, 20, 21, 27, 29, 51, 54, 63, 76, 83, 95
Wrigley, William, Jr., 39, 46, 57, 85, 89

About the Author

JOHN A. MORELLO is a History Professor in the Department of General Education at DeVry Institute of Technology, Addison, Illinois.

THE UNIVERSITY OF MICHIGAN

DATE DUE

APR 3 0 2004

APR 1 4 2004